ECOLOGY
AT THE
HEART OF
FAITH

ECOLOGY AT THE HEART OF FAITH

DENIS EDWARDS

ORBIS BOOKS

Maryknoll, New York 10545

Sixth Printing, April 2011

Founded in 1970, Orbis Books endeavors to publish works that enlighten the mind, nourish the spirit, and challenge the conscience. The publishing arm of the Maryknoll Fathers and Brothers, Orbis seeks to explore the global dimensions of the Christian faith and mission, to invite dialogue with diverse cultures and religious traditions, and to serve the cause of reconciliation and peace. The books published reflect the opinions of their authors and are not meant to represent the official position of the Maryknoll Society. To obtain more information about Maryknoll and Orbis Books, please visit our website at www.maryknoll.org.

Cover art, "Arctic Tale" by Susan Seddon-Boulet (1941 – 1997), used with permission of Eric Boulet.

Library of Congress Cataloging in Publication Data

Edwards, Denis, 1943-
    Ecology at the heart of faith / Denis Edwards.
        p. cm.
    Includes bibliographical references and index.
    ISBN-13: 978-1-57075-665-8 (pbk.)
    ISBN-10: 1-57075-665-1
    1. Human ecology—Religious aspects—Christianity. 2. Stewardship, Christian. 3. Theology. I. Title.
BT695.5.E49 2006
261.8'8—dc22

                                                    2006013129

Printed on recycled paper

Grace

The names of Beauty fail this pulse of revelation
    unworded, unknown it overruns the centuries
Like a swan upon the wind where the flood of light
    begins

Swooping to the depths where tyrants twist our tongues
    it teaches us to smile
    away our fear of love
    and rhymes our heartbeats to a deathless dawn

So where do we begin and how do we receive
    such a precious gift
    reaching us complete
    with every breath we breathe?

Like dolphins in the waves we are carried home to You.

Peter Edwards (1951-1994)

Contents

Acknowledgments

Generous colleagues and friends have read and commented on this text and I am grateful to each of them. Alastair Blake has long been a valued dialogue partner not only because of his perspective as a physicist but also because of his theological insights. Beth Prior, chief librarian of the Adelaide Theological Library, read the manuscript with a keen eye for what communicates to readers as well as for the theology. Patricia Fox read it from the perspective of someone whose focus is the theology of God. While working on this book I have been a member of the Advisory Council of Catholic Earthcare Australia and I am thankful for all who have been involved with this group, and particularly to Col Brown and Trish Hindmarsh for reading the manuscript and giving me their thoughtful reflections on it. They form part of the community of discourse from which this text springs.

This is meant to be a "user-friendly" book that brings together and builds on earlier work I have done in specific areas of ecological theology. Chapter 2 is a development from *Made from Stardust* (CollinsDove, 1992). Chapter 3 reflects *Breath of Life: A Theology of the Creator Spirit* (Orbis, 2004). Chapter 4 has echoes of *Jesus and the Cosmos* (Paulist, 1991) as well as *Jesus the Wisdom of God: An Ecological Theology* (Orbis, 1995). Chapter 5 picks up some ideas from *The God of Evolution: A Trinitarian Theology* (Paulist, 1999) and from "The Diversity of Life and the Trinity," *Interface: A Forum for Theology* (May 2004), 94-100.

Chapter 6 contains ideas worked out in a paper presented to the Karl Rahner society of the Catholic Theological Society of America in 2005, entitled "Resurrection of the Body and Transformation of the Universe in the Theology of Karl Rahner," awaiting publication in *Philosophy and Theology*. It makes use of ideas discussed in the article "Every Sparrow That Falls to the Ground: The Cost of Evolution and the Christ-Event," which is to be published in *Ecotheology* 11 (March 2006). Chapter 7 contains some material developed in "Celebrating Eucharist in a Time of Global Climate Change," *Pacifica* 9 (February 2006). The general approach of the book was articulated in "Ecology at the Heart of Christian Doctrine" in *The Australasian Catholic Record* 81 (January 2004).

Special thanks to Bill Burrows and to all at Orbis Books for their generous work on this book and their ongoing commitment to theology in a global context.

1

Introduction

One of the gifts we have received from the twentieth century is a picture of Earth as our shared home. The human community of the twenty-first century can see Earth as a blue-green planet set against the darkness of interstellar space. We are able to think of our home planet in the context of the vast distances of the Milky Way Galaxy and of the roughly one hundred billion galaxies that make up the observable universe, and be led to a new appreciation of Earth's beauty and hospitality to life. We can see human beings as part of a global community, interconnected with other species and with the life systems of our planet. This represents a precious new moment in human cultural history.

At the same time we are confronted by the damage human beings are doing to the atmosphere, the soil, the rivers, and the seas of Earth. It is becoming more and more obvious that if we continue to destroy the great forests and clear the bush, if we continue reckless exploitation of the land, the rivers, and the seas, if we continue to lose habitats, what we will pass on to our descendants will be an impoverished and far more sterile place. We are in the midst of a process that, if allowed to continue, will end in the destruction of much of what we have come to treasure.

Everything is interconnected. The continued use of fossil fuels, like the vast amounts of coal mined in my own land, Australia, contributes to rapid climate change that will bring terrible suffering to human beings and a further acceleration in the extinction of other species. Already uncounted and unnamed species are being lost forever. All of this will have an unimaginable impact on human beings, but it is also obviously far more than a human problem. At the center of this book is the argument that this loss of biodiversity is a *theological* issue. When human beings cause the extinction of other species, they destroy creatures made by God. They damage a mode of God's self-revelation.[1]

Ecological Conversion

As the sense of the global crisis deepens, there is a growing movement of people committed to finding an alternative way forward, an ecological movement. It is made up of people from diverse backgrounds—farmers, artists, scientists, trade unionists, business leaders, school children, and politicians, among many others. They are connected in a common love for the Earth and its creatures. I am convinced that this movement, along with the interrelated movements committed to justice for the poor of the Earth and to the full equality of women, represents a central way in which the Spirit of God is at work in our world today.

Religious faith has an important contribution to make to the ecological movement. It can give meaning and motivation, build an ecological ethos, and contribute to the foundations of an ecological ethics. For many people around the globe religious faith continues to provide fundamental meaning. For such people, ecological commitment can receive its deepest grounding only at a religious level. For those who belong to the Christian community, ultimate meaning is found in the idea that God is with us in Jesus of Nazareth and in the grace of the Holy Spirit. This means that the fundamental task of a Christian ecological theology is to show the inner relationship between faith in Jesus of Nazareth and ecological commitment.

Important steps have been taken by individual churches as well as by the World Council of Churches. The Ecumenical Patriarch of the Orthodox Church has regularly brought people together to learn about contemporary ecological issues and to reflect on them in dialogue with theologians. In the Roman Catholic world, Pope John

Paul II insisted that respect for the integrity of creation is a moral issue, and he introduced the important theme of *ecological conversion*. While lamenting the fact that humanity has failed God in its abuse of the planet, he celebrates the beginning of a conversion to ecological awareness and action:

> If one looks at the regions of our planet, one realizes immediately that humanity has disappointed the divine expectation. Above all in our time, humanity has unhesitatingly devastated wooded plains and valleys, polluted the waters, deformed the earth's habitats, made the air unbreathable, upset the hydrogeological and atmospheric systems, blighted green spaces, implementing uncontrolled forms of industrialization, humiliating—to use an image of Dante Alighieri—the earth, that flower bed that is our dwelling. It is necessary, therefore, to stimulate and sustain the *"ecological conversion"* which over these last decades had made humanity more sensitive when facing the catastrophe towards which it was moving.[2]

This movement of ecological conversion is far wider than the church. It involves people from all kinds of ethnic, political, and religious backgrounds. In this movement, Christians are called to humbly take their stance alongside others, many of whom have long led the way in ecological conviction and practice. However, the church has its own specific task in this movement of conversion. It is called to witness to the God of Jesus Christ, and to this God's love for all Earth's creatures. In this process, the church itself is called to ecological conversion.

Commitment to ecology has not yet taken its central place in Christian self-understanding. It is far from central in terms of structure, personnel, and money. As the church itself is called to conversion to the side of the poor in the struggle of justice and to the side of women in their struggle for full equality, so the church itself is called to conversion to the side of suffering creation. Christians are called to play their part precisely as Christian believers, alongside others, in the far wider movement of conversion that the Spirit of God is stirring up in the community of humankind.

Ecology and Christian Faith

The argument of this book is that Christians will be able to play their own particular role in this movement of the Spirit only by coming to a new understanding of the ecological meaning and consequences of their deepest faith convictions. Some Christian thinkers who are strong and important advocates for ecological conversion have argued that Western Christianity's emphasis on traditional doctrines needs to be replaced by more emphasis on creation theology or creation spirituality. So, for example, Thomas Berry turns from aspects of the mainstream Christian tradition toward broader creation spirituality and to a new story of the universe.[3] Matthew Fox seeks to replace what he sees as a dualistic Augustinian fall–redemption theology with a theology of original blessing and of the cosmic Christ.[4]

It is not my intention to enter into a critical analysis of the thought of these authors. There is much in their work to learn from and much with which I agree. My intention is simply to point to a specific way in which I will take a different approach. I will propose a theological response to the ecological crisis not in terms of bypassing central Christian traditions but in terms of going *more deeply* into them and seeking to reinterpret them in the light of the ecological issues that confront us. I will argue that this Christian heritage, above all the living memory of Jesus as God-with-us bringing healing and liberation, is deeply connected to creation. It is important to acknowledge that there are many instances where Christian tradition has been expressed, interpreted, and lived in an exclusively anthropocentric (human-centered) way. With the authors mentioned above, I see it as part of the task of ecological theology to take a critical stance toward all interpretations of this heritage that exalt the human at the expense of other creatures.

The heart of the Christian tradition has to do with a God who gives God's self to us in Christ and the Spirit. It is a message of redemption and hope that cannot be abandoned by the church but is always to be proclaimed in new ways in new times. I will argue that it carries within itself potential for being critically reinterpreted in an authentic ecological theology for the twenty-first century. Only such a theology will enable Christians to see their ecological commitment in its most radical context. Such a theology has a role in persuading the wider Christian church that following Jesus Christ in the twenty-first century involves the call to ecological conversion.

My proposal is that when the great themes of Christian faith are approached in a way that is critical but respects them in all their beauty and depth, they hold a great deal of promise for an emerging ecological theology. With Lutheran theologian H. Paul Santmire, I will be seeking to explore what he calls the "ecological and cosmic promise" of Christian theology.[5] I am convinced that exploring the heart of Christian faith can open out into a great deal of ecological meaning, precisely because the God that Christians find revealed in Christ and the Spirit is the God who creates the universe. The God of redemption is the God of creation. What is being offered here is very much a partial view, limited among other things by my own specific location as an Australian who is male, ordained, and relatively wealthy by global standards.

As it is the responsibility of Christians to explore the ecological meaning of Christianity and in this way to contribute to an ecological ethos and commitment, so, I believe, it is for those belonging to other traditions, including Jewish, Muslim, Buddhist, Hindu, and Confucian believers, to bring out the ecological meaning of their traditions. It is demanded of all of us that we listen to the ancient indigenous religious traditions of the peoples of Australia, and to traditions of many other peoples that involve a profound respect for the land and for all its creatures. The global community of Earth needs the contributions of all the great religious traditions of our planet. A common commitment to creation by people from different religious faiths can offer real hope for the future of life on Earth.

Methodologically, I will start from below, from what it is to be human in the midst of creation (chapter 2), and then move to the experience of the Spirit (chapter 3), before turning explicitly to consider the place of Jesus in ecological theology (chapter 4). The chapters on the Spirit and on Jesus open out into an ecological theology of the Trinity (chapter 5). This will lead to reflections on the final transformation of all things in Christ (chapter 6) and on worship and practice (chapter 7). At every stage I will work from the perspective of the Christ-event. While these six issues are at the heart of Christian faith, they do not cover the whole content of faith,[6] and I make no attempt to develop an ecological ethics.[7] What is offered here is meant as a limited work of constructive theology, an attempt to reinterpret some fundamental aspects of the Christian tradition in the new context we face in the first part of the twenty-first century. In each chapter, then, I will offer an interpretation of a fundamental theme of Christian faith in relation to the other themes developed in this book and attempt to bring out and to make explicit its ecological meaning.

2

Human Beings within the Community of Life

"Made in the Image of God"

A key issue for an ecological theology is its understanding of human beings and their interconnection with other creatures. How is the human person to be seen in relation to plants, insects, birds, and animals, and to the land, the seas, and the atmosphere that support and nourish life? Any contemporary theology of the human, above all one that claims to be ecological, will need to situate the human within the community of life. It will need to be a theology of the human-in-relation-to-other-creatures.

Scientific cosmology and evolutionary biology offer fundamental resources for an ecological theology of the human. They tell us a story of the human that was not available to theologians of the past. They situate the human in relation to the history of the universe and the history of life on Earth. A Christian theology of the human will not only learn from the sciences but also build on the resources of the Christian tradition concerning the identity of the human being before God. At the center of this tradition, I will propose, is the idea that humans are made in the image of God (the *imago Dei*) and stand always before God's gracious self-offering love.

In what follows, I will begin by tracing the story of human beings as it is told by contemporary science: humans are born from the Big Bang, made from stardust, and part of a three-and-a-half-billion-year history of life on Earth. Then I will explore the Christian tradition's notion of the human being within the community of creation as made in the image of God. Finally I will ask about the theological relationship between human beings and other creatures. After exploring four possible approaches, I will propose a concept of the human that involves *both* kinship with other creatures and the call to cultivate and take care of creation.

Born from the Big Bang

One of the most far-reaching discoveries of the twentieth century is the idea that our universe is not static but expanding dynamically. Galaxies are moving away from one another at an increasing rate as the universe stretches and expands. Cosmologists can now trace the observable universe back to a time about fourteen billion years ago when it was unimaginably small, dense, and hot.[1] They call the theory that describes the emergence of the universe from the first fraction of a second after it came into existence the Big Bang. The Big Bang theory does not describe what happened at time zero.[2] Ordinary physics breaks down before it reaches this point. According to influential theories in cosmology, within the first fraction of the first second, the universe went through a period of inflation—extremely rapid expansion.

Scientists are more confident in describing what happened from the first second onward. Cosmologists like Martin Rees insist that cosmology can give a reasonable scientific account of the emerging universe from the end of the first second.[3] By this time, ordinary particles such as protons and neutrons and electrons already existed. As the universe expanded and cooled, the nuclei of the simplest element, hydrogen, and of some of the helium, were formed. Hydrogen was the first element formed, and it remains the dominant element in our universe. At this stage it was still far too hot for the nuclei of hydrogen and helium to form into atoms. There was rapid transformation of energy between matter and radiation, and particles and radiation were coupled together. By the end of the first three minutes, the observable universe existed as an expanding and cooling fireball, made up of the nuclei of hydrogen and helium.

When the universe was about four hundred thousand years old, it became cool enough for nuclei to bond with electrons to form atoms of hydrogen and helium. In this process, matter was de-coupled from radiation. The universe became transparent to the great sea of radiation that fills it. This is the cosmic microwave radiation. Thirteen and a half billion years later, in 1965, this back-ground microwave radiation would be discovered by Arno Penzias and Martin Wilson. Scientists now studying this radiation find that it gives them a snapshot of the early universe. It is a remnant from the primordial fireball.

We human beings are also, in our own way, remnants of the fire-ball. Along with all the other creatures of Earth, we have a heritage that goes back to the Big Bang about fourteen billion years ago. Hydrogen is a fundamental element in the structure of the cells of all living things; and when combined with oxygen, it forms the water that fosters and sustains life. We are inescapably constituted by and continually depend on the hydrogen that is born in the events of the early universe. The history of the universe is our history. In this real sense we are children of the early universe.

The human community on Earth and all the other species of our planet sprang from the primordial fireball. It carried within itself the potentiality for the universe we see around us. It contained within itself the possibility of all that would ever emerge, including the Milky Way, our solar system, Earth, and all its diverse creatures. Human beings, along with all the other creatures in the life commu-nity of Earth, are the unfolding of the potential already contained within the great primordial blaze of energy.

Along with the Christian tradition, I am convinced that every-thing in the universe exists only because it is continuously created by God. But Christian faith does not tell us *how* the universe emerges and develops. Here theology needs to listen to science. A theology that listens to science will see God as creatively at work in and through the whole process of the emergent universe described by contemporary cosmology. It will see God as empowering the emer-gent universe, and every aspect of it, from within. God creates in such a way that all the potentialities of the universe emerge from the primeval events.

This leads to the initial formulation of an important insight about God, one that I find confirmed in what we know about subsequent events in the story of the universe and of life: *It is characteristic of God to create in an emergent and evolutionary way.* God creates human beings as emergent creatures: We are born of the universe, constituted of the hydrogen atoms that emerged in the early universe fourteen billion years ago.

Made from Stardust

It takes more than hydrogen to make a human being. We are a carbon-based form of life. The molecules of our bodies are composed of atoms of carbon, hydrogen, oxygen, and nitrogen, with small amounts of other elements. While the hydrogen atoms come from the early universe, the carbon, oxygen, and nitrogen all come from the stars. The story of the emergence of stars is a central part of the human story.

As the universe expanded and cooled, slight unevenness in density meant that there were locations where large clouds of hydrogen accumulated. These gas clouds were the beginning of the galaxies of our universe. Under the influence of gravity, pockets of gas were compressed and heated up until they reached the extremely high temperatures at which nuclear fusion reactions can occur. Then the first stars were born, lighting up the universe.

A star is a thermonuclear furnace in which hydrogen is converted into helium. When the hydrogen is exhausted, further nuclear reactions can convert helium into heavier elements, including the carbon, nitrogen, and oxygen from which we are made. Very large stars end in supernova explosions that produce still heavier elements, seeding the nearby universe with elements for the formation of further stars and their planets.

Astronomer John Barrow says that it takes something like ten billion years of stellar burning to produce the carbon and the other elements from which our bodies are made.[4] Two to three generations of stars are needed to provide chemicals for the dolphins, koalas, and human beings of Earth. Every atom of all the elements found naturally on Earth, apart from the primordial hydrogen, has its origin in a star. Each carbon atom in the blood flowing through my veins and in the neurons firing in my brain comes from a star. We are made from stardust.

In a recent book, astronomers George Coyne and Alessandro Omizzolo speak of the "social" character of the universe. They point out not only that the more abundant chemical elements in our bodies came from three generations of stars but also that some less abundant elements may come from millions of distant galaxies.[5] We are radically interrelated with the universe. Martin Rees speaks of a "galactic ecology" of our home galaxy, the Milky Way. It is a wonderfully abundant storehouse of raw materials for life. Rees points out that a carbon atom in a cell of a human brain has a pedigree that extends back before the birth of the solar system 4.5 billion years ago. Atoms now gathered in a single strand of human DNA would, billions of years ago, have been widely dispersed in different stars spread around the galaxy or in interstellar space.[6]

The interstellar clouds of the Milky Way Galaxy contain complex organic molecules and amino acids that are fundamental to the emergence of life on Earth. John Gribbin explains how they got here: "The raw materials from which the first living molecules were assembled on Earth were brought down to the surface of the Earth in tiny grains of interplanetary material, preserved in the frozen hearts of comets from the interstellar debris of the giant molecular cloud from which the Solar System formed."[7] Life on Earth can be understood only in relation to organic material that comes from the stars via the comets that collided with the emerging planet in its formative period.

All of this points to a close interrelationship between human beings and the universe, its galaxies, and stars. This interconnection is brought out even more sharply in what scientists call the cosmological "anthropic principle." This points to the fine-tuning of the universe that is required if it is to be one in which humans can emerge.[8] Without precisely the right balance between the expansive force of the universe and gravity, galaxies could never have formed. And without just the right level of irregularity or clumpiness in the early universe, they could not have come into existence. Without galaxies, there would be no stars and no living creatures.

The anthropic principle points to the close relationship between the age and size of the universe and human emergence. The universe needs to have been expanding for something like fourteen billion years if galaxies are to form, stars are to ignite, elements like carbon are to be synthesized, a solar system incorporating these elements is to be formed around the sun, and human life is to evolve on Earth. Frogs and eagles depend on this fine-tuning of the universe just as much as human beings do. We are all interconnected in the one story of the universe, and we are all made from stardust.

Emerging within Evolutionary History

Earth and the other planets begin to form around the young sun about 4.5 billion years ago. Within about a billion years, life appears on Earth in the form of bacterial cells. These are simple structures without a nucleus (called *prokaryotes*). The emergence of bacterial life and of the self-replicating DNA molecule is an enormous step in our history, one that is not yet fully understood by science. The next big step is the emergence of single-celled creatures that possess a developed nucleus (the *eukaryotes*). They make the evolution of more complex organisms possible. Biologist Ernst Mayr has recently argued that eukaryotes may have evolved as early as 2.7 billion years ago. He sees this evolutionary step as "arguably the most important event in the whole history of life on Earth."[9]

Developed multicellular animals (known as the Ediacara Fauna) appear in the fossil record from about 570 million years ago. Life takes new forms in the seas of the Cambrian period (545-495 million years ago). Animals become bigger, developing robust shells and skeletons, and the first vertebrates move onto land about 375 million years ago. Most forms of marine life are lost in the enormous extinction of 248 million years ago. Dinosaurs, flying reptiles, marine reptiles, and mammals appear during the Triassic (248-206 million years ago) and Jurassic (206-144 million years ago) periods. Birds and flowering plants emerge at the beginning of the Cretaceous period (144-65 million years ago). The extinction of 65 million years ago wipes out more than half of Earth's species. Life evolves in new ways, with mammals diversifying and flourishing in new habitats.

Between eight and five million years ago, chimpanzee-like apes established themselves in the tree savannah at the edge of the African rain forest, developing a two-legged style of walking. According to the calculations of molecular biologists, the last common ancestors of humans and modern apes lived between seven and five million years ago. Various hominid species (the *Australopithecines*) evolved between four million and two million years ago. There was an increase in brain size in some species, called *Homo*, such as *Homo rudolphensis*.

Homo erectus emerges about two million years ago with a large brain and an athletic body and soon spreads from Africa to other parts of the world. These early humans use fire, design stone tools, and can run like modern humans. They evolve into various groups including the Neanderthals, who flourish between 250,000 and 30,000 years ago. It seems likely that modern humans evolve from *Homo erectus* in Africa about 150,000 years ago. They are lighter than *Homo erectus*, but possess a much larger brain. They spread from Africa to the world, reaching Australia about 60,000 years ago.

We human beings share a common history of life with all the other creatures of Earth. We carry within us a story of life that goes back to our pre-human ancestors in Africa, back to the trilobites of the Cambrian seas, and ultimately back to the first bacterial forms of life 3.5 billion years ago. This story is part of the larger story of the universe itself. The human community is born of the Big Bang, made from stardust, and part of the evolutionary history of life on Earth. This story forms a basis for a theological view of the human being. The other essential basis for a Christian theology of the human being within creation is the Christian tradition itself. How does this tradition illuminate the story of the emergence of the human? The next section begins to respond to this question, and the rest of the book will continue the discussion.

Image of God

The Christian community has upheld the unique dignity of the human person with the ancient biblical concept of the human being, male and female, as made "in the image of God" (Gen 1:27). In my view this is a precious part of the Judeo-Christian heritage, one that is not to be lightly put aside. It provides the foundation for a Christian view of the radical value of each person before God. It is the basis for the Christian commitment to equal and mutual relations between women and men, to just economic and social relations, and to peaceful resolution of international conflicts. I believe it needs to have a place in an ecological theology that also seeks to be a theology of interhuman justice.

This concept of the human as image of God becomes dangerous when it is used to set humans up in opposition to other creatures, above all when it is used to suggest that humans have absolute and unlimited rights over other species. I believe that a critical ecological theology must reject this use of the image of God as a destructive distortion, but I will propose that it is possible to retrieve this powerful biblical idea in an ecological theology that situates human beings in relationship to other creatures, and that understands each creature as in its own way reflecting and imaging God. While the Bible and the Christian tradition use the language of image of God specifically of the human, they also see the whole of creation, and the diversity of life on Earth, as the self-expression of God and, in this sense, as imaging God. As I hope to make clear in chapter 5, an eagle in flight, a wildflower in its delicate beauty, an ecosystem, and the biosphere of Earth can each in its own way be seen as a self-expression of the Creator, and thus as an image of God.

In the New Testament, Jesus Christ is seen as the image or, in the original Greek, as the *icon* of God. Paul speaks of Christ as "the image of God" (2 Cor 4:4) and sees others as conformed to this image by grace (Rom 8:29; 1 Cor 15:49; 2 Cor 3:18). The hymn to Christ in the Letter to the Colossians sings of Christ as the "image of the invisible God" (1:15). Jesus is the true icon, the one in whom all things are created and the one in whom all are reconciled. Jesus risen, as the true image of God, is the firstborn of *all things* in creation. The concept of the *imago Dei* transcends the human. It applies to the risen Christ, as the true image in whom all creatures find salvation and new life. It has universal meaning. Christ Jesus is the image of God not just for human beings but for all creatures. In him the reconciliation of all things has begun.

While recognizing this universal role of Christ as the true image of God, the Christian community has usually used the image language for human beings to bring out the uniqueness of humans before God. Some theologians of the early church, like Irenaeus, distinguished between "image" and "likeness." They used "image" to refer to humanity created by God and "likeness" for what occurs when human beings are conformed to Christ through grace. Others, like Athanasius, spoke of Jesus Christ as the true "image" and others as, by grace, "according to the image" that is Christ.[10] What is it about the human that is in the divine image? There has been a tendency to locate the image of God in one aspect of the human, such as the human soul, the capacity for reason, or free will. Some recent thinkers have located what is unique to humans in their self-consciousness. In earlier work, I have followed Karl Rahner's view of the human being as creation come to self-consciousness, able to respond to the Creator in freedom and love.[11] While I still find some truth in this as a general description of human evolution, I have become convinced that there are dangers in any exclusive focus on self-consciousness. If self-consciousness is used to define the human, above all before God, it can appear to deny humanity to those who live with psychological disabilities.

What finally makes us unique before God is not any one capacity we possess or any partial aspect of the human. It is the whole human being understood *as personal and as interpersonal.* Being created as the *imago Dei* means that God creates human beings as persons in order to embrace them in *interpersonal* love. God, of course, can be thought of as embracing in love and promising final fulfillment to persons whose own capacities are limited by illness or disability. Biblical scholar Claus Westermann interprets the phrase "image of God" in Genesis as indicating that humans are creatures with whom God is able to engage personally. They are creatures to whom God can speak (Gen 1:28, 29-30).[12] Theologian Karl Barth describes the image of God as involving the "confrontation and reciprocity" of an "I" and a "Thou."[13]

While Barth emphasizes the human in contrast with other creatures, I see this interpersonal relationship between Creator and human creatures as occurring precisely in the midst of, and in relation to, the rest of creation. Christian theology of creation understands God as relating to all creatures in ways that respect their specificity, integrity, and proper autonomy. In this context, what is specific to the human can be seen as the personal, the capacity to go out from oneself to the other in interpersonal love. Precisely this personal dimension of the human involves the human in relationship not only with that radical other who is God, and not only with other human beings, but with the others who are our fellow creatures. Precisely because human beings are made in the image of God, they are called like God to care for every sparrow that falls to the ground. They are called to love their fellow creatures as God loves them, not in sentimental and anthropomorphic ways, but in a way that respects the distinctiveness and otherness of a kangaroo, an eagle, or a whale.

To be called into relationship with the living God is to be invited into a world of grace, a world in which God is present to each person in self-offering love. One of the truly great gains of twentieth-century theology is the clarity it achieved about the universality of God's self-offering in grace.[14] In this view of grace, all have the possibility of responding to God's self-offering. All have the possibility of salvation in Christ. The Spirit of God, the Spirit who is always the Spirit of Christ, is understood as present with human beings from the very beginning. But the Christian tradition maintains that if human history is a history of grace, it is also a history of sin, of a rejection of God that enters into the place of human freedom. We tend to be curved in upon ourselves in destructive ways. We dominate and exploit one another and abuse other creatures, regardless of the consequences. We make war on one another and destroy the life systems of the planet. We live in alienated and damaging ways. All of this constitutes a need for wholeness and healing, for liberation and forgiveness that the Christian community finds in Christ.

Human beings are made in the image of God in the sense that they are made for interpersonal love. A mountain range, a brilliant parrot, a great soaring tree, a delicate wild flower bending in the wind—these too are images of God. They are the self-expression of God, sacraments of divine presence in the world. They image God in their own specificity. But the precise specificity of the human is the personal and the relational, and this involves the human in the vocation to relate to other creatures as God does.

While all creatures are held in the creative love of God at every moment, human beings are embraced by this love in an interpersonal way. They are creation come to personhood, and as persons they can thank and praise God on behalf of the rest of creation. In this sense, Orthodox theologians rightly speak of human beings as called to be "priests of creation."[15] They "lift up" creation to God. As part of the community of creation, human beings are to celebrate God's creation and to praise God on behalf of creation. Their vocation is to love this Earth as God loves it and to delight in the diverse creatures of our planet as God delights in them. To be made in the image of God involves loving and respecting the integrity of each creature with Godlike love and respect.

Kinship with Creation—Cultivation of Creation

I have been proposing that human beings are born from the Big Bang, made from stardust, and part of the evolutionary story of life on Earth. Within the community of creation, they are made in the image of God in the sense that they are called into an interpersonal relationship with God in grace and to graceful relations with their fellow creatures. What needs more careful exploration at this point is the relationship between human beings and other creatures.

In the opening chapter of Genesis, God is presented as delighting in the diversity of creatures and declaring them all to be good: the light, the seas, the dry land, seed-bearing plants, fruit trees, sun and moon, sea creatures and birds, cattle, creeping things, and wild animals of every kind. All the abundance and fruitfulness of creation come from God, who blesses all creatures and says, "Be fruitful and multiply and fill the waters in the seas, and let birds multiply on the earth" (Gen 1:22). The exuberance of life springs from the blessing of the Creator. At the end of the sixth day, after the creation of humans in the image of God and the declaration of their dominion over other creatures, we are told, "God saw everything that he had made, and indeed it was very good" (Gen 1:31).

In the second chapter of Genesis, the newly formed human being is told to "cultivate and care for" what God has given (Gen 2:15).[16] Later, after the flood, the Creator enters into an eternal covenant with Noah that embraces every living creature (Gen 9:12-16). The rainbow is to be the enduring sign of this covenant with all living things. In the Psalms, God is seen as the one who sustains and nourishes all living things: "You make springs gush forth in the valleys; they flow between the hills, giving drink to every wild animal" (Ps 104:10-11). It is God who gives the breath of life to every creature: "When you send forth your spirit they are created and you renew the face of the ground" (Ps 104:30). The variety of creatures manifests and expresses the beauty and wisdom of the Creator: "O Lord, how manifold are your works! In wisdom you have made them all; the earth is full of your creatures" (Ps 104:24).

In this broad biblical vision, God creates each creature, sustains its existence, delights in its goodness, and blesses it with fertility. Human beings are a part of God's creation, interrelated with all other creatures yet called to act responsibly before God within creation. In these texts and in many others, the Bible sees all creatures in relationship to God. It offers a fundamentally God-centered (*theocentric*) vision of reality rather than a human-centered (*anthropocentric*) one. I propose that this biblical theocentric vision forms the appropriate framework for further development of an ecological theology of humans in relationship to other creatures. I will work toward my own position by considering four models of or approaches to this issue: domination of nature; ecological egalitarianism; kinship with creation; and cultivation of creation.

Domination of Nature

Some Christians hold explicitly or implicitly that nature is there simply for human beings to exploit. They see human beings as having the right to dominate creation and to use it for their own benefit, without limits or constraints. In the past, such an exploitative approach to nature has been supported by an assumption that the resources of nature are limitless. While few would hold this view today, governments, companies, and individuals act as if they have every right to exploit nature without regard for the cost to future generations of human beings or to other creatures. Large corporations act on this principle, seeing themselves as accountable only in terms of profits for their shareholders. The result is accelerated global climate change; pollution of land, seas, and air; and the tragic loss of biodiversity.

Those who seek to justify human domination and exploitation of creation sometimes invoke the Bible. It is not difficult to take texts out of context and use them for this purpose. It must be admitted that not all biblical texts are Earth-friendly. Texts such as the command to "have dominion" over other creatures and to "subdue" the Earth (Gen 1:28) can be used to legitimate ruthless exploitation.[17] In itself, this biblical language is harsh, and it becomes dangerous in the extreme when it is co-opted to serve the exploitative interests of an industrialized world. This dominion text has become a symbol of the way in which Christianity has contributed to the crisis we face. In 1967, Lynn White charged that the ecological crisis could be attributed in large part to Christianity.[18] While I think this challenge was overstated, it has led to healthy critical responses in the emerging discipline of ecological theology. There can be no doubt that Christians have often failed in their responsibilities to creation and have been guilty of uncritical anthropocentrism, and that those who exploit nature ruthlessly have been able to misuse biblical texts to justify their positions. While Christianity has to accept some responsibility for the ecological crisis, a list of major contributors would need to include the Enlightenment view of the natural world in instrumental terms, the rise of capitalism, the industrial revolution, technological society, an economy based uncritically on endless growth, uncontrolled corporations, and unrestrained greed.

The command of Genesis to "have dominion" over other creatures comes from an ancient context where nature could seem alien and terrifying to ordinary, humble, relatively defenseless human beings. It comes from a time when, in the creation narratives of peoples who were neighbors of Israel, human beings were born to be slaves of the gods. By contrast, Genesis points to the human vocation as a "kingly" one of bringing human intelligence, courage, and work to bear on the land so that herds might flourish and crops might grow. In a Jewish world, this kingly role was understood in the context of God's shepherding rule and God's love for and delight in all creatures. In the Christian community, Jesus' life and death stand as a radical critique of all dominating views of power and authority (Mark 10:42-45). It is unfaithful to the wider biblical tradition to interpret the "dominion" text as supporting the ruthless exploitation and the domination of nature by large corporations in our day.

The model of domination is destructive and false. I believe it must be absolutely rejected in an ecological theology of human beings in relation to other creatures. It does not respect the biblical heritage of the goodness of creation, the community of all creatures before God, the call to humans to act as images of God, or the divine command to cultivate and care for creation (Gen 2:15). The World Council of Churches and many Christian churches have rejected as false the idea that human beings have unlimited rights to exploit or damage the natural world. According to Christian social teaching, human beings have moral duties toward the natural world. They do *not* have absolute rights over nature. Pope John Paul II, for example, taught that human beings must respect the integrity of other creatures and the integrity of ecological systems. He insisted that in relation to other creatures we are constrained not only by biological laws but also by *moral* laws.[19] In a God-centered perspective, other forms of life have their own God-given value. They have value in themselves, intrinsic value, a value that human beings are called to respect.

Ecological Egalitarianism

If the model of domination of nature represents an extremely anthropocentric approach, one that has been all too pervasive and destructive, its opposite is an approach that tends to reject any special or unique place for humans. It finds expression in the work of the Norwegian philosopher Arne Naess. He introduced the concept of "deep ecology," which he sees as undermining the dominant paradigm that privileges the place of humans in the biosphere. He speaks of an "ecological egalitarianism" and of a "core democracy" in the biosphere.[20] These views are widely represented in ecological discussions and are influential in some forms of ecological theology and creation spirituality.

Those who take this position embrace a biocentric (life-centered) approach rather than an anthropocentric one. They rightly oppose the human exploitation that is bringing death and extinction to so many other species. They rightly argue for the intrinsic value of other creatures. They rightly urge a far humbler stance from human beings. Many who hold this view have led the way in ecological commitment and action. There is a great deal that Christian theology can learn from people who hold this position.

However, the tendency to claim that all creatures have equal value and that there is no special place for the human is problematic for a Christian ecological theology. It undermines the biblical view of the uniqueness of the human. If taken in an absolute sense, it fails to provide grounds for discernment between the moral value of a bacterium and that of a human person. In abandoning the uniqueness of human beings made in the image of God, it undermines a fundamental basis for the struggle for social justice. This view also undermines a powerful source of ecological commitment. Human beings have a unique moral responsibility for other creatures. There is a unique moral demand made upon them to respond urgently, creatively, and wisely to the ecological crisis they have created.

Kinship within a Community of God's Creatures

The model of human beings as kin to other creatures within a community of creation is based on the biblical notion that there is one God who continually creates all the diverse things that exist, delighting in their goodness (Gen 1:31) and embracing them in covenant love (Gen 9:12-16). In the Christian tradition, this idea finds particular expression in the spirituality of Francis of Assisi (1182-1226), the patron saint of ecology, and in the theological tradition that is associated with him. Francis saw God's creatures as interconnected in one family of creation. He sang, in his *Canticle*, of other creatures as sisters and brothers to us. This *Canticle* is not simply an expression of naïve piety, but a deliberate and highly successful attempt by Francis to communicate a kinship approach to creation at a popular level.[21] Later I will refer to the work of Bonaventure (1221-1274), a key figure in the Franciscan tradition, who understood the variety and diversity of God's creatures as expressing the beauty and abundance of the trinitarian life of God.

Contemporary Christians have much to learn about kinship from the traditional cultures of indigenous peoples. Theologian Wali Fejo, an Indigenous Australian from the Larrikia country around Darwin, writes:

> My people are the original custodians of the land in this part of Australia. We look after the land as we look after a mother. And the land looks after us like a mother. From the land comes our law and our life, our stories and our strength. Our own land is also within us and binds us to the place where we live. Even when we are displaced or taken away and seem to have lost our roots, the land stays within us. The task is to find ourselves by finding the land within and making the connection with our country. We are "heirs" to the land spiritually, just as Christians say they are heirs of Christ. Wherever I go I have a piece of land within me.[22]

For Wali Fejo, and for his people, the crocodile is kin—an attitude that I must admit I find hard to share at this stage. However, coming to terms with the otherness of crocodiles is part of coming to terms with wilderness. It is part of the ecological conversion to which we are called.

Ian Barbour points out how contemporary science also offers support to a kinship model. He argues that everything in nature is interconnected. At the level of physics, the atoms in human brains have a cosmic story in common with the atoms in plants and animals. At the level of biology, we human beings share a common family tree in the evolution of life with all the other creatures of Earth. More than 99 percent of our active genes are identical with those of chimpanzees.[23]

Theologically, I would propose that this kinship brings into play what I have identified as the image of God in the human, the personal. It involves humans as persons, personally connecting with other creatures, respecting and loving them in all their differences from ourselves. It does not make other creatures into human persons, but engages with them as they are. Paul Santmire rightly argues for such a truly personal relationship between human beings and nature. He takes up Martin Buber's "I–Thou" concept, proposing that the human relationship with nature is to be seen as far more than an "I–It" relationship. Santmire has no intention of making nature into a human person, but seeks to go beyond objectifying nature as an "it." He argues for an extension of Buber's personalism to include nature as a mysterious other to which a human "I" can relate. In this sense, he argues for "relationships of mutuality between persons and other creatures of nature."[24]

Mutuality is a theme that appears also in the work of ecofeminist theologians like Rosemary Radford Ruether. She argues for "a spirituality and ethic of mutual limitation and of reciprocal life-giving nurture, the very opposite of the spirituality of separation and domination."[25] Elizabeth A. Johnson is a strong advocate of the kinship model between human beings and the rest of creation. She writes of deep interconnections within a community of creation: "Woven into our lives is the very fire from the stars and the genes from the sea creatures, and everyone, utterly everyone, is kin in the radiant tapestry of being."[26] Dawn Nothwehr, building on both feminist theologians and the Franciscan tradition, argues for mutuality as a central norm for a Christian environmental ethics. She sees human beings as radically relational, as called to reciprocal and loving relationships with each other and with other creatures before a relational God.[27]

I believe that this kinship model is the essential foundation of a truly ecological theology of human beings in relation to other creatures. It challenges the model of domination and exploitation. Adopting the kinship model demands a form of *conversion*. It involves a new way of seeing and acting. It involves extending the love of neighbor to embrace creatures of other species. It involves extending the love of enemy to involve creatures that confront us as other and inspire fear in us. It involves loving and valuing others as

God loves and values them. Ultimately, it is a God-centered (theo-centric) view of an interconnected community of creatures that have their own intrinsic value.

Cultivating and Caring for Creation

Although I propose that this kinship model is foundational for a contemporary ecological theology of the human in relation to other creatures, I believe something more is needed. By itself, kinship does not point clearly enough to human responsibility within the Earth community. It has little to say to human creativity. Just as human ingenuity has been used to plunder the natural world, so humans can use their God-given creativity and intelligence to bring healing to the Earth and its creatures, human and nonhuman. Alongside the Franciscan attitude to creation there is the older tradition associated with St. Benedict (ca. 480-547). In this tradition, love for God's creation takes the form of responsible farming and preservation of the land. It also involves the love of learning and the conserving of a precious cultural heritage. Over many centuries, Benedictine spirituality has given expression to the biblical injunction "to cultivate and take care of" (Gen 2:15) the good things of God's creation.

I prefer the biblical language of "cultivating and caring for" to the language of "stewardship," which is biblical only in the loose sense of being based on some of the New Testament parables, whose primary focus is the kingdom of God. Of course, the language of stewardship can be used meaningfully to point to human responsibility for creation before God. But when stewardship is used to characterize the human stance before other creatures, it can run the risk of suggesting an inflated view of the human as a necessary intermediary between God and other creatures. It can seem to suggest that other creatures do not have their own relationship with the living God or their own integrity.

The language of cultivating and caring for creation can include the many ways in which human creativity is used for the good of the community of life on Earth. It includes not only farming with best land-care practice, but also cooking, gardening, building, painting, doing science, teaching, planning, taking political action and many other creative actions. What is crucial is that cultivating and caring for creation *are based on the conversion implied in the model of kinship*, a conversion in which human beings come to see themselves as interrelated in a community of life with other creatures, a community in which each creature has its own unique value before God.[28] In this context, human creativity stands humbly before other creatures, respecting their right to exist and to flourish and committing itself to their conservation and flourishing.

At the deepest level, such a human stance before the rest of creation is about wisdom. Wisdom is a unique form of knowledge. It does not seek to grasp or to control. It respects the mystery of the other. It is a form of loving knowledge that involves humility and wonder before the natural world. It involves loving the creatures God loves. It also involves recognizing human finitude before the mystery of God and the mystery of creation. This is the stance found in Job, when God is presented as addressing Job from the whirlwind: "Where were you when I laid the foundations of the earth? Can you bind the chains of the Pleiades, or loose the cords of Orion? Do you know where the mountain goats give birth? Did you give the horse its might? Is it by your wisdom that the hawk soars, and spreads its wings towards the south?" (Job 38:4-39:26).

As called to cultivate and take care of creation, human beings are part of the unfolding of creation, called to participate responsibly in the dynamism of ongoing creation. We are intimately linked to the life-forms of our planet, and to the atmosphere, the soil, and the oceans. Our existence is encompassed by the mystery of God revealed in all the variety of creatures that surround us. We are part of them and they are part of us. All of us together reflect the limitless divine love that is our origin. We are born of the universe, made from stardust, part of evolutionary history of life on Earth and, as such, made in the image of God and kin to all the wonderfully diverse plants, insects, birds, and animals of our beautiful planet, and called to cultivate and care for the Earth and all its creatures.

3

The Creator Spirit

"Giver of Life"

How is the life-giving Spirit connected to the world of whales, kookaburras, and grevilleas? It seems that many people have a sense of the Spirit at work in the natural world, yet a fully ecological theology of the Creator Spirit is seldom articulated. Even when, in the creed, we Christians affirm faith in the Holy Spirit as the "Giver of Life," there seems little connection between this life-giving Spirit and the ecological issues that confront us.

This chapter will explore an ecological theology of the Holy Spirit. It will begin with a brief outline of the biblical theology of the Spirit as the life-giving Breath of God, and then offer a theological approach to the story of the Spirit as a big story that involves creation, grace, incarnation, and church. This will lead to reflections on the Spirit as the power of God at work in evolutionary emergence, as companioning creation in its groaning, and as the unspeakable closeness of God in creation.

Breath of God

In the Bible, the English word "spirit" is used to translate the Hebrew word *rûaḥ* and the Greek *pneuma*. Both of these words have the meaning of "breath" and "wind." Behind the biblical idea of the Spirit of God there is the image of the Breath of God. In some ancient biblical texts, the Breath of God simply refers to a unique or particularly powerful quality in a human being. In others, it points to the creative and renewing presence and action of the one God of Israel. The Breath of God expresses the power of God at work in creation, in ecstatic prophecy, in the rise of kingship and, later, in messianic expectation. It refers to the life-giving and empowering presence of God in nature, in the history of Israel, and in the lives of individual human beings.

In a number of passages, the Spirit is thought of as the Breath of Life. Creatures live only because God gives them this life-giving Breath. In Genesis, God forms the first earthling from the dust of the ground and breathes into the human's nostrils "the breath of life" (Gen 2:7). Because of this breath of life, the earthling "became a living being." Human beings live only so long as they have the divine breath abiding in them (Gen 6:3). The great flood will "destroy from under heaven all flesh in which is the breath of life" (Gen 6:17; 7:22). Those to be saved go into the ark with Noah "two of all flesh in which there is the breath of life" (Gen 7:15).

In the Book of Job, Elihu says: "The spirit of God has made me, and the breath of the Almighty gives me life" (Job 33:4). A little later, he declares of all living things: "If he should take back his spirit to himself, and gather to himself his breath, all flesh would perish together, and all mortals return to dust" (Job 34:14-15). In the great image of Ezekiel, the Breath of God enables dry bones to be brought to life (Ezek 37:9; Eccl 12:7). Psalm 104 sings of all God's creatures: "When you take away their breath, they die and return to their dust. When you send forth your spirit, they are created; and you renew the face of the ground" (vv. 29-30).

The images of breath and word are closely interlinked—our human words are carried on our breath. In the biblical tradition, creation is attributed to both God's creative Word and God's life-giving Breath. Psalm 33 explicitly links the two images together in the one divine act of creation: "By the word of the Lord the heavens were made, and all their host by the breath of his mouth" (v. 6). The same connection is made in the Book of Judith: "Let all your creatures serve you, because you spoke, and they were made. You sent forth your spirit, and it formed them" (16:14).[1]

For the first Christian communities, this is the same Spirit, the same Breath of Life, who overshadows Mary at the conception of Jesus (Matt 1:18; Luke 1:35), anoints Jesus at his baptism (Mark 1:10), and is poured out on the Christian community at Pentecost (Acts 2:4). In Paul, we hear that this Holy Breath dwells in Christians, adopting them into the divine life, and enabling them to pray "*Abba!* Father!" (Rom 8:15). In John, we are told that the Spirit is given to Christians as their personal Advocate who will remain with them forever (John 14:16).

While the First Testament presents the Spirit as the life-giver in many ways, including in the biological sense, the Christian writings see the Spirit as life-giver in a new sense—as the bearer of resurrection life: "If the Spirit of him who raised Jesus from the dead dwells in you, he who raised Christ from the dead *will give life* to your mortal bodies also through his Spirit that dwells in you" (Rom 8:11). Paul associates the risen Christ closely with the Spirit. He speaks of Christ as the new Adam who "became a *life-giving spirit*" (1 Cor 15:45).[2] In John, we are told that no one can enter the kingdom of God without being born again from the Spirit (John 3:5). Jesus speaks of the Spirit as a spring of living water welling up from within (4:14; 7:39). After the discourse on the Bread of Life, Jesus proclaims that "it is *the spirit that gives life*" (6:63). Building on these texts, the Nicene-Constantinopolitan Creed would express the faith of the Christian community in the Holy Spirit as "the Giver of Life."

In both senses, that of creation and new creation in Christ, the Spirit of God is the life-giver. The great theologians of the East, such as Irenaeus, Athanasius, and Basil, always see the Word of God and the Breath of God as involved *together* in creation and redemption. They constantly return to the words of the Psalmist: "By the word of the Lord the heavens were made, and all their hosts by his breath" (Ps 33:6). Irenaeus images the Word and Spirit as the "two hands of God" at work in creation and salvation.[3] In the West, Ambrose of Milan develops a theology of the Creator Spirit as the creative power of God who not only brings things into being but also brings all things into harmony and beauty. He sees the Creator Spirit as the author of both creation and the incarnation: "So we cannot doubt that the Spirit is Creator, whom we know as the author of the Lord's incarnation."[4]

The Big Story of the Creator Spirit

In spite of Ambrose's insight into the role of the Holy Spirit in creation and incarnation, these fundamental dimensions of Spirit theology have often been overlooked. Many Christians think of the Spirit as coming at Pentecost, with little sense of the Spirit's work in creation, grace, and incarnation. The focus is so much on the great event of Pentecost that the rest of the story of the Spirit is forgotten. What is needed is to rediscover the much bigger story of the Spirit.

In what follows, I will suggest that the full story of the Spirit involves not simply the one episode of Pentecost but four great episodes: *creation, grace,* the *Christ-event,* and *Pentecost.* It needs to be remembered that even these four episodes are far from the whole story of the Spirit, since the Spirit of God is the eschatological Spirit, the one who brings all things to their final fulfillment in Christ.

Creation

The theological story of the Spirit of God begins long before Pentecost, long before Moses led the people of God from slavery, long before Abraham and Sarah were called to leave their home in Ur and journey into the unknown, and long before the first hominids appeared in Africa. The story of the Spirit's work in our world embraces the universe itself. The Creator Spirit is the dynamic, energizing power of God enabling our observable universe to exist and to evolve from the first moment of its existence fourteen billion years ago. If, as some cosmological models suggest, our observable universe has its origin in relation to a much larger universe, or multiverse, then theology would see this unthinkably enlarged universe as God's creation and as the work of the Creator Spirit.

At the end of his *Brief History of Time*, Stephen Hawking asks a famous question: "What is it that *breathes fire* into the equations and makes a universe for them to describe?"[5] Christian theology has a response to this fundamental question. It claims that it is the Creator Spirit, the life-giving Breath of God, who breathes fire into the equations that describe our universe. It sees this Creator Spirit as the immanent power of ongoing creation (*creatio continua*) that enables a universe of creatures to exist, evolve, and flourish.

In this theological vision, the Spirit empowers the dynamics of the early universe, the emergence of the first stars that lit up the universe thirteen billion years ago and the formation of our solar system around the young sun 4.5 billion years ago. The Spirit works creatively in the physical processes, seemingly delighting in emergence and complexity in the pre-life universe. This Spirit is the energizing power of continual creation who breathes life into the emergence of bacteria, eukaryotes, multicellular creatures, land animals, plants, hominids, and modern humans. The Spirit is creatively at work in the whole process, celebrating every emergence, loving life in all its diversity and treasuring it in its every instance.

Grace

The Creator Spirit who breathes life into creation is also the bringer of grace. Grace is a word that can mean different things to different people. I am using it to refer to the idea that God freely offers God's self in love to a human being. Grace, then, is God. It is what traditional theology called uncreated grace (God) as opposed to created grace (the created effect of God in us). It is God inviting a human being into interpersonal love. To say yes to this offer is to be embraced in divine love. To be embraced by God is to be liberated and transformed, to become a participant in the very life of God. In traditional language it is to be saved, to be justified in Christ.

The Christian tradition has held that this grace is given to us in Christ, through his life, death, and resurrection. It has always associated the free gift of grace with Christ, but has also struggled to understand what this meant for people who were not Christian. Over the last two thousand years there has been a good deal of confusion over this issue. In the last chapter I pointed to the important clarification of church teaching concerning grace that occurred in the Second Vatican Council. It proclaimed that God's saving grace is not confined to the church but reaches out in the Spirit to all people. More recently, Pope John Paul II has returned to this teaching, insisting that this saving work of Christ in the Spirit is truly universal, including all who lived before Christ: "*We need to go further back,* to embrace the whole of the action of the Holy Spirit even before Christ—*from the beginning,* throughout the world, and especially in the economy of the Old Covenant."[6]

There is a long story of grace that precedes the historical events of the life of Jesus, going right back to the beginning of human existence on Earth. When human beings emerge in evolutionary history, they emerge into a Spirit-filled universe. They emerge into a world that is filled with the Spirit of God. The Creator Spirit, who had always been lovingly present to every creature in the relationship of *creatio continua,* is now present to human beings in an *interpersonal way,* meeting them in the depths of their personal life in self-offering grace. The Creator Spirit, then, is not only the life-giver but also the grace-bearer.

Human existence is always a story of grace—at least in the sense that grace is always offered. Alongside this story of grace, of the Spirit ever-present to human beings in self-offering love, there is a story of willful rejection of grace, a long history of sin that enters into the place of human freedom and inclines to sin. Human beings are born into a world of grace, but are also drawn toward lovelessness, ruthlessness, and violence. In the midst of such a world, the Spirit offers freedom and salvation in a way that Christians understand as anticipating, and as directed toward, the Christ-event. The Spirit present in self-offering love to every human being and the Word of God made flesh in Jesus of Nazareth are united together in one divine "economy" of saving love. Word and Spirit are distinct aspects of God's one act of self-giving to human beings and to creation, but they are always interrelated.

The story of the Spirit is a story of God present with, accompanying, and celebrating every form of life. When humans emerge in the history of life, they emerge into a world that is filled with the Spirit. This Spirit not only enables the emergence of the human but delights in humans as creatures who can respond to divine self-offering love in a fully personal way. Human beings emerge in a world of grace—in the sense that they come to exist in a world where God embraces them in the life of the Spirit. They exist before a God who constantly offers God's very self to them. From the beginning, humans are offered the gift of transforming and sanctifying grace by the Spirit who is the bearer of the grace of Christ.

The Christ-Event

The Spirit of God, present in every aspect of the emergence of our universe, with every atom, and every distant galaxy, with every living creature from bacteria to dinosaurs, is present by grace to all human beings. This grace-bearing Breath of God leads the people of Israel throughout their sacred history. In the Christ-event, this same Spirit brings about the incarnation, sanctifying and transforming the humanity of Jesus, so that he can be Word of God, the human face of God in our midst.

Mark begins the story of Jesus with his baptismal anointing by the Spirit and with the words from heaven: "You are my Son, the Beloved; with you I am well pleased" (1:11). Luke and Matthew take us back to the conception of Jesus. In Matthew, we hear twice that Mary the mother of Jesus "was found to be with child from the Holy Spirit" (1:18, 20). In Luke, the angel says to Mary: "The Holy Spirit will come upon you, and the power of the Most High will overshadow you; therefore the child to be born will be called holy; he will be called Son of God" (1:35). The creeds that emerged in the early church point to the central role of the Spirit in the incarnation. In the Apostles' Creed we find: "He was conceived by the power of the Holy Spirit and born of the Virgin Mary." The Nicene-Constantinopolitan Creed states: "By the power of the Holy Spirit he became incarnate."

With the Christian sources testifying so clearly to the role of the Holy Spirit in the Christ-event, it is hard to explain how this fundamental idea became somewhat obscured in much Western theology. It has been recovered in recent times, in the work of theologians like Walter Kasper, who understands the Spirit as sanctifying the humanity of Jesus, making it possible for him to be God's loving self-communication in person.[7] Kasper and other contemporary theologians are attempting to retrieve and develop a theology that, as I noted in the last chapter, was grasped in the fourth century by Ambrose, in his teaching that the Holy Spirit is "the author of the Lord's incarnation."[8]

The Gospels present Jesus not only as anointed by the Spirit but also as open to the Spirit and led by the Spirit in every aspect of his life and ministry. Yves Congar has insisted that in the life of Jesus we need to see a true *history* of the Spirit.[9] Jesus invokes the Spirit in the specific circumstances he faces and is led by the Spirit in new ways as he confronts these particular situations. Above all, Jesus is open to the Spirit in a radical way in the dark night of the cross, but that is not the end of the story. The same Spirit transforms the brutal violence and suffering of the cross into an event of redemptive love. The risen Jesus, now radically identified with the life-giving Spirit in the glory of resurrection life, pours out the Spirit upon the church in the Pentecost event.

Pentecost

The Spirit who breathes life into creation, who enfolds human beings in grace, and who brings about the Christ-event, is poured out on the community of disciples at Pentecost, constituting them as the church of Jesus Christ. This means that the church exists from both the risen Christ and from the Spirit. Word and Spirit co-institute the church.[10]

While Eastern Christians have maintained a living sense of the place of the Holy Spirit in the life of the church, the Western churches have tended to focus exclusively on Jesus Christ. We Christians of the West are experiencing a need to rediscover the Holy Spirit, to learn again to invoke the Spirit and to expect the Spirit to lead the church in new ways. We are being invited to become a church that seeks to discern what the Spirit is asking of it in new contexts. This discernment will involve an openness to the new. It will be an attempt to listen to the promptings of the Spirit in the "signs of the time" in the light of prayerful reflection on the living memory of Jesus.

As Jesus was led by the Spirit at every stage of his life, so the church must be led by the Spirit. This means constantly invoking the Spirit and being open to the new in the Spirit. A theology of the church in which the Spirit is given a proper place will involve a renewed understanding of the *charisms* that are foundational for the whole life of the church, including its structure and ministry.[11] These charisms are gifts of nature and grace given for the fulfillment of the mission of the church—such as those of preaching, teaching, healing, music, art, peacemaking, and prophetic words and deeds on behalf of human liberation. In our own day we might well add the charism of ecological witness and action.

Congar insists that charisms are given to all members of the church. He points out that this means that the church can be open to the Spirit only when it is open to the charisms of each member: "The Church receives the fullness of the Spirit *only in the totality of gifts made by all her members*."[12] If the church is to listen to what the Spirit is saying in all its members, this will require effective participatory structures in church life. We need to think of the church, Congar says, not as "ready-made," but as always in the process of being built by the Spirit of God. It is the Spirit of God who will lead the church into its unforeseeable future.

This big story of the Spirit, a story that involves creation, grace, incarnation, and church, is still far from complete. It will not be completed until all things are taken up in the risen Christ. The

Breath of God draws us into the new, into the openness of God's future. The Spirit thus appears as God-before-us. This Breath of Life, creatively present in all creatures, draws Christians beyond the church into communion with the whole of creation. Living in the Spirit in the life of the church is to be exposed to the life-giver who creatively embraces all the diverse forms of life on Earth. As Jürgen Moltmann has said, the experience of the "communion of the Holy Spirit" (2 Cor 13:13) takes the church beyond itself into the communion of all God's creatures.[13]

The Creator Spirit in the Emergence of an Evolutionary World

We belong to a universe that is expanding and evolving, a universe that is in dynamic process, where complex entities are formed from simpler components. What is remarkable is that, while complex things evolve from what already exists, something radically *new* can emerge, with properties that cannot be reduced to what was there before.

When life emerges on Earth, it depends on atoms and complex molecules that already exist. Yet in relation to what was there before, it is radically new. The first bacterial forms of life had characteristics that cannot be reduced to their component molecules. When human beings emerge with a developed brain, language, and culture, something radically new appears on Earth. How can this emergence of the new be understood? It is the role of science to seek explanations for emergence at the empirical level. But theology has its own role to play. Its task is to ask about God and God's creative action in an evolutionary and emergent universe.

Karl Rahner has contributed to a new theology of creation for an emergent universe. He thinks of God creating through a process of active self-transcendence in creatures. To transcend means simply "to go beyond." Rahner's proposal is that we think of God as continually at work in the universe as it evolves and emerges, and as continually giving creation *itself* the capacity to become something new, to become more than it was. Rahner works out his theology of self-transcendence in relation to his Christology, and this will be discussed in the next chapter.[14]

In relation to the theological story of the Spirit advanced in this chapter, I think it is faithful to the biblical and theological tradition to see the Creator Spirit, always in the communion of the Trinity, as the immanent presence of God who empowers the process of self-transcendence and the emergence of a life-bearing universe. At the deepest level, beyond the level of scientific explanation, the life-giving Spirit of God enables creatures to become. This Creator Spirit is the immanent divine power of evolutionary emergence. The Wisdom of Solomon taught long ago that the Spirit is the creative divine principle in all things (Wis 12:1), and this insight is once again being recovered in our time by a number of theologians. Catholic theologian Walter Kasper, for example, writes that the Holy Spirit is at work "whenever something new arises, whenever life is awakened and reality reaches beyond itself, in all seeking and striving, in every ferment and birth."[15] And Lutheran theologian Wolfhart Pannenberg says simply, "the Spirit of God is the life-giving principle, to which all creatures owe life, movement, and activity."[16]

The Spirit of God is the dynamic presence of God to creatures, enabling them to exist and to evolve by embracing them in relationship with the divine communion and drawing them toward their future in God. The Spirit is the power of becoming, the Life-Giver who enables the evolutionary emergence of the life-forms of Earth in all their fruitfulness and diversity. In the emergence of life and of human beings, as well as in many other instances, something radically new happens. Creation transcends itself. There is reason to hope that science will continue to grow in its capacity to account for these emergences. Theology operates at another level, asking: What is it that breathes life into the process and enables a universe of creatures to exist and to evolve into what is new? It sees the Creator Spirit as the one who enables the self-transcendence of creation from within. It sees the Spirit as the Life-Giver, who, always in the communion of the Trinity, goes forth and fills creation as the power of *continuous creation* (Job 33:4; 34:13-15; Wis 1:7; 12:1).

The Spirit in the Groaning of Creation

The long history of life on Earth is not only a history of fruitfulness, beauty, cooperation, and symbiosis but also a history of creatures preying on other creatures. It involves competition, death, and the extinction of species. Death is intrinsic to the pattern of biological life. Evolution can occur only through a series of generations, and this necessarily involves the death of individuals. Death is the price paid for the evolution of eyes, the wings of birds, and the human brain.

Science has taught us to think about ourselves as coming to be only as part of an evolving universe and the evolution of life on Earth. We are so much the result of an evolutionary world that we have no realistic way of thinking about human beings, and the other creatures of Earth, apart from evolution with all its costs. What is obvious is that if creation took another form, the universe could not be the kind of universe it is, the living creatures of Earth could not be the creatures they are, and we human creatures could not be the evolutionary creatures we are. It is also clear that it is only the existence of consistent laws in nature that allow science to work. If there was no consistency in nature, if it did not follow regular laws, or if God were a God who intervened arbitrarily in nature, science could not function.

More than any other generation we know that the costs of evolution, including pain and death, are built into the process of the evolution of life. For those who believe in a Creator, the conclusion is inescapable—God has chosen to create through emergence and evolution with its associated costs. The ancient question arises: If God is good and all-powerful, why does God create in this way? Theology does not have a complete answer to offer. It stands before a God of incomprehensible and uncontrollable mystery. It can only ever make a humble human attempt at articulating what can be said about a God who transcends limited human concepts and words. Christianity cannot claim to have the whole picture about God's purposes and God's action in creating. It does not know why creation takes the shape it does.

Christians are convinced, however, that the incomprehensible God has come close to us in Jesus. On the basis of this self-revelation of God in Christ, some profoundly important things can be said: that God is a God of radical compassion and love, that in the cross God enters into and embraces the suffering of a suffering world, that death is not the final meaning, and that God is a God who brings life out of death. Building on these revelatory insights, I will take up three lines of thought: divine power as a power-in-love, the Spirit's embrace of a suffering world, and the Spirit transforming this world from within.

Redefining Divine Power as Power-in-Love

If the Creator Spirit can be seen as the immanent presence of God to creation, as the one who breathes life into the whole process of ongoing creation, and as the power of God at work in the self-transcendence of creation, it becomes crucial to ask: What kind of power is this? Christians have long affirmed belief in God as all-powerful, or as omnipotent. It is not my intention to question this assertion, but to affirm it. It rightly points to the power of God at work in creation and in the resurrection of Jesus Christ. On the basis of this power, Christians hope for a future transformation of all things in Christ. What needs to be questioned is the *nature* of the power that is attributed to the Creator. I think that what is often at work when God is described as all-powerful is the idea of a despotic human ruler, one who can overrule anyone and anything. The image of divine power comes from the model of a human tyrant who can do absolutely anything, no matter how arbitrary or ruthless, with no regard for the consequences to others.

With other theologians in recent times, I believe it is essential for

Christians to redefine divine power in terms of the Christ-event. Divine power is certainly revealed in Jesus of Nazareth, but it is revealed in a specific and confronting way. The Gospels present Jesus as rejecting and forbidding the dominating forms of power exercised by tyrants. The only power that Jesus will allow in his community is that of mutual service and mutual love, which will find its most radical expression in the cross and resurrection (Mark 10:42-44; Matt 20:24-28; Luke 22:24-27; John 13:1-15). Paul tells his community at Corinth that Christ *crucified* is "the power of God and the wisdom of God" (1 Cor 1:24). In the crucified one, divine power may look like foolishness and weakness, but, Paul insists, "God's weakness is stronger than human strength" (1 Cor 1:25). Divine power is revealed in the vulnerability of the crucified. In Philippians, the Christian community is urged to take on the mind of Christ Jesus, who emptied himself to the point of death on a cross (Phil 2:3-11). Something extremely powerful happens in and through this self-emptying. Jesus is exalted and God's purposes are achieved in a way that is contrary to all human views of power.

The love revealed in the cross is extreme in its vulnerability, but it is also filled with the power of life. It is in the vulnerability of love "for others" to the end that resurrection power breaks in upon creation. The cross and resurrection redefine divine power. As Walter Kasper points out, they reveal that divine omnipotence is the transcendent power to give oneself in love. It is radically power-in-love. It is not that God strips God's self of power on the cross: "On the contrary, it requires omnipotence to be able to surrender oneself and give oneself away."[17] The cross and resurrection reveal the true nature of divine power. It is revealed as the infinite capacity for self-giving love, a love that does not overpower but works in and through creaturely processes to bring life. It enables the integrity and autonomy of the other. This differs radically from all understandings of power as the capacity to dominate others.

God's power is revealed in Christ as a power-in-love, as a relational power. This suggests that the very *nature* of divine power is that it enables the other to flourish in all its integrity. Human experience of love, at its best, can offer some hints about the nature of divine love. One who loves authentically does not dominate the other, but has the capacity to make room for the other. Those who love in this way can freely let go of themselves without fear of losing themselves. They can receive others into the space of their own lives and their own hearts. They can allow the other to be themselves, to claim their own integrity and autonomy. It seems that all genuine human loving involves some level of vulnerability. The human experience of vulnerability in love can offer an analogy for the kind of divine power in love that is at work in the Christ-event. God can be thought of as having the capacity for loving in vulnerability to the other, *in an utterly transcendent and divine way.*

I am arguing that the nature of the power revealed in the cross of Christ should be what governs all Christian thinking about God as all-powerful. Because God is consistent and faithful, we can expect that this same kind of divine power will be at work in creation and final consummation. If divine power is redefined in the Christ-event as involving respect for and vulnerability before the integrity of creaturely freedom and creaturely processes, then this suggests that it may be appropriate to think of the Creator Spirit as freely respecting not only the integrity of human beings but also the integrity of natural processes. It has always been held in Christian theology that God can act only in accordance with the divine *nature,* and this nature has always been understood as love. If this divine nature is revealed to us in the cross, then it would seem that God's actions, which will always be true to the divine nature, will respect the integrity of creatures and creaturely processes.

If the Creator's love and respect are not limited to the human but embrace all creatures, including the processes that govern the emergence of the universe and the evolution of life on Earth, then God may be committed to respect the unfolding of creation according to its own proper laws. If divine action in creation is understood in terms of love that respects the integrity of the other, then the divine power at work in the evolving universe is not the capacity for arbitrary, ruthless, or overpowering action. It is nothing like that of an absolute human tyrant. If the Spirit is freely committed to the proper autonomy of creaturely processes, then this life-giving Spirit may be committed to respect the integrity of natural processes.

Loving Companion to Each Creature

In the cross of Jesus, Christians find a God who enters into the pain of the world, who suffers with suffering creation. In the resurrection they find a promise that death does not have the last word. The Christ-event points to a God who not only feels *with* suffering creation, but who is already at work transforming suffering into life. It points to something that is not obvious from a reflection on creation in all its beauty and ambiguity—that God is a God of boundless and overwhelming love and compassion, a compassion that reaches out to every human being and to every sparrow that falls to the ground (Matt 10:29; Luke 12:6).

On the basis of revelation, and only on this basis, Christians can see the presence of the Spirit to each creature as the presence of boundless love. Each entity in the universe exists only because it is embraced by the Creator Spirit in the relationship of ongoing creation. This creative embrace is an act of love. Creation is nothing else but the dynamic presence of the Spirit in the love that enables entities to exist and to become in a dynamic interrelated world. On the basis of the faith of Israel, the author of the Wisdom of Solomon was already convinced that God creates only in love:

> For *you love all things that exist*,
> And detest none of the things that you have made,
> For you would not have made anything if you had
> hated it.
> How would anything have endured if you had not
> willed it?

Or how would anything not called forth by you have
    been preserved?
You spare all things for they are yours, O Lord,
You *who love the living.*
For your immortal spirit is in all things.

                    (Wis 11:24–12:1)

Creation springs from love. Because God loves each creature, the Spirit dwells in it, enabling it to exist within the community of creation. The Spirit of God is the faithful companion to each creature, present to every creature in the universe, accompanying each with love, valuing it, bringing it into an interrelated world of creatures, holding it in the dynamic life of the divine communion. God is present, in the Spirit, to each creature here and now, loving it into existence and promising its future.

Creation is an act of love. Ruth Page has argued that God is to be understood as companioning each creature with love that respects each creature's own identity, possibilities, and proper autonomy. Each creature in its uniqueness, with its own life, its own beauty, its own suffering, matters to God. As Page points out, this conviction has immediate ecological consequences. If God knows and cares about each creature's experience, God also knows and cares about each creature's habitat.[18] The Spirit is grieved (Eph 4:30) when human beings abuse and destroy habitats.

God really does know every sparrow that falls to the ground (Matt 10:29; Luke 12:6). As Rosemary Ruether says, each being "has its own distinct relation to God as source of life." This means that each has its value: "Each life form has its own purpose, its own right to exist, its own independent relation to God and to other beings."[19] If God really does care about every sparrow, every ant, every great white shark, every creature hunting another for food, and every creature that is the prey of another, then Christianity has its own position on the value not only of species but also of individual creatures. Many scientific ecologists rightly focus on populations and species and their interaction with their environment. Christian theology also needs to focus on individual creatures as the object of divine love and as creatures in which the Spirit of God dwells.

The Spirit as Midwife to the Birth of the New

A Christian response to the suffering of creation necessarily involves eschatology. It looks to the future when all things will be taken up into God and transformed in Christ. This will be the theme taken up and developed in chapter 6 of this book. At this point it is important to note that the work of the Spirit is always directed toward this future transfiguration of the whole of creation. Something is being born in the labor of creation that we can only glimpse from our limited perspective. But we do experience the Spirit at work in ourselves, and in this experience, Paul tells us, is the beginning and the guarantee of the transformation of creation in Christ.

Paul sees creation as waiting with "eager longing" for its liberation from "bondage to decay" and for "the freedom associated with the glory of the children of God" (Rom 8:19-23). The Spirit assists and enables the birth of the new: "For we know that the entire creation has been groaning together in the pangs of childbirth up till now" (8:22). This suggests that the Spirit can be understood not only as the companion of creation in its travail but also as the midwife to the birth of new creation. It is always the life-giving Spirit of God who enables the new to be born. In this sense the Spirit is not only midwife but also the one who empowers the process from within. The Spirit is the "down payment and guarantee" (2 Cor 1:22; 5:5; Eph 1:13-15), the "firstfruits" of God's harvest (Rom 8:23). If the Spirit is the midwife to the new creation, this points toward the unimaginable: the participation of all creatures in the dynamism of the divine life.

A theology of creation in the light of the cross and resurrection suggests that the Creator Spirit may be lovingly committed to the proper autonomy and independence of creaturely processes. It sees this Spirit as *with* creatures in their finitude, death, and incompletion, holding suffering creatures in redemptive love, and as drawing each into an unforeseeable future in the divine life. For the Christian community, the experience of the Spirit is an anticipation of the eschatological communion of all things in God. This Spirit is present with each creature now, with every wild predator and with its prey, with every expression of life and in every death, as midwife to that birth in which all things will be made new.

The Spirit as the Unspeakable Nearness of God in Creation

The Christian tradition sees the Word of God as revealed in the humanity of Jesus, in the human face of Jesus. By contrast, it does not see the Spirit as having a human face. The Spirit is revealed as the far more mysterious Breath of God, breathing through the whole of creation and through the lives and hearts of human beings. This Spirit searches everything, "even the depths of God" (1 Cor 1:10). The creative Breath of Life is present to our universe in countless ways that are far beyond the limits of the human. The biblical images for the Spirit tend to come from the natural world: breath, wind, living water, fire, and anointing with oil. These images preserve the otherness of the Spirit of God and resist the human tendency to domesticate the Spirit.

Long ago, Ambrose saw the Spirit sweeping over the waters of creation not only as the Life-Giver to all things but also as the one who brings beauty to creation. The great medieval mystic Hildegard of Bingen (1098-1179) saw the Spirit as the source of *viriditas*, a Latin word that means greenness and points to the fruitfulness and the abundance that are at the heart of life on Earth. More recently, the theologian Jürgen Moltmann (1926-) has spoken of the Spirit as the "unspeakable closeness of God" in creation.[20] Moltmann's phrase captures something of the human experience of the Spirit in encounters with the natural world. The Holy Spirit is the unspeakable closeness of God in the experience of mountains, deserts, forests, and seas, in the sense of being deeply connected with a place, and in moments of real encounter with trees, flowers, birds, and animals.

The presence of the Spirit in the otherness of the nonhuman is a direct challenge to the anthropocentrism that sees God as focused only on the human. It stands opposed to all attempts to use religious faith to legitimate the ruthless exploitation of other species. It points to the otherness of nonhuman creatures as a place of God. One of the characteristics of the biblical understanding of the Spirit of God is that this Spirit remains wild and uncontrollable. The Spirit cannot be domesticated. It is the wind that "blows where it chooses" (John 3:8).

We can glimpse the wildness of the Spirit in the experiences we have of wilderness in nature. We can encounter this wild Spirit not only in deserts and rain forests but also in the mysterious and counterintuitive nature of quantum reality. We come up against the mystery of the Spirit when we ponder the nuclear furnaces burning in stars and struggle to imagine our observable universe with its fourteen-billion-year history and its more than one hundred billion galaxies.

The experience of wilderness in all its forms can lead to a deepened sense of the incomprehensible and uncontrollable Spirit of God. And dwelling in this Spirit can lead us to a new respect for what is wild and beyond human domestication. The Spirit is not only the love that stirs in the intimate depths of our own beings, but is the love that surrounds and sustains the uncounted insects, animals, and trees that share the exuberant life of a rain forest. The acceptance of the presence of the Spirit in what is untamable can be an important step in the emergence of an ecological sensibility that can value the diversity and otherness of the creatures who share life with us.

Although the Spirit is clearly not to be thought of as a human person, this does not mean that the Spirit is *less* personal than human beings. The Spirit can be thought of as personal in a way that wonderfully transcends the human way of being person. The Spirit is radically relational. The Spirit of God is "the love of God poured out in our hearts" (Rom 5:5), and this divine love is present to us as the mysterious depth of all human love. This presence, in which we live and move and have our being, is not a something. It is not simply a link or a bond uniting us with God or each other. The Holy Spirit is a personal presence, a mysterious other, a Thou, someone to be loved and worshiped. The Spirit of God is not less than humanly personal but infinitely more.

4

Ecological Commitment and the Following of Jesus

Making the connection between ecological commitment and Jesus of Nazareth is at the center of a Christian ecological theology. This connection is not something that can be taken for granted. It is far from obvious to many people that ecology has anything to do with Jesus. Numbers of Christians who are deeply committed to ecology find it easy enough to see their commitment in relation to God as Creator, but they cannot see a connection with the story of Jesus.

It is an urgent task for theology to show the interconnection between the living memory of Jesus and the issues that confront the global community. Only when this connection is made will ecological action be seen not only as ethically responsible but also as radically Christian, as the faithful praxis of Christian discipleship. Only then will the wider Christian community be challenged from within its own Christian depths to ecological conversion.

According to the Gospel tradition, Jesus embodies the compassion of God in his person, his words, and his actions. He offers healing and hope to those suffering illness and exclusion. He brings liberation and joy to those imprisoned by psychological bonds. He invites women as well as men into the circle of his followers to form a new family of sisters and brothers. He interprets God's gift of the *Torah* in terms of compassion. He announces forgiveness for sinners and celebrates festive meals with public sinners and outcasts that anticipate God's coming reign. He teaches that love is the meaning of everything—love for God with one's whole self and love for one's neighbor as oneself. He insists that this love has no limits. It can have no borders. It is to embrace the enemy.

In the limited and finite life of Jesus there is unleashed an explosive dynamism of compassion that knows no boundaries. This is evident in every aspect of Jesus' ministry, but it reaches its radical expression in the absolute dark night of his death and in the disciples' experience of Jesus as the risen one. In encountering Jesus beyond death, the disciples discover that the compassion of God manifest in Jesus cannot be contained by the tomb, but breaks free as a dynamic power of liberation and hope. In a way that remains ever mysterious, the utter humiliation, ugliness, and brutality of the cross has become a spring of compassionate life flowing out into the whole world. What flows forth is nothing less than the dynamic Spirit of God.

In all of this, the first Christians become convinced that a new stage in God's salvation history has been reached. They see what has occurred in Jesus as having universal meaning. The unstoppable dynamism of the Spirit leads them beyond the boundaries of Jesus' own ministry, which had been centered on Israel. In the power of the Spirit, the disciples come to understand that fidelity to the God revealed by Jesus now demands a new universality. Divine compassion is directed to the whole world. It reaches out beyond the human community to embrace "all things" in the reconciliation of Christ (Col 1:15-20).

Through the ages, Christian saints and sages have recognized that this divine compassion does not stop with human beings. Paul told the first Christian community in Rome that the whole creation awaits its redemption in Christ (Rom 8:19-24). At the end of the second century, Irenaeus saw the whole of creation as recapitulated (summed up and transformed) in Christ and as destined to share in Christ's victory over death. In the thirteenth century, Francis of Assisi showed how the divine compassion embodied in Jesus reaches out to embrace individual animals and birds as brothers and sisters to us before God. In the early twentieth century, Pierre Teilhard de

Chardin came to see the whole of evolutionary history as empowered by the risen Christ, the Omega who is the source and goal of the whole emergent process.

Christians who reflect on Jesus today, from the perspective of the twenty-first century, do so as participants in a human community engaged in the extinction of uncounted species of living creatures. This context challenges us to think again about the compassion of God revealed in Christ and its relationship to the nonhuman creatures of our global community. In this chapter, I will begin to take up this issue from what we know about Jesus' own attitude to creation. This will be followed by some reflections on the way that the first Christians understood Jesus in relation to creation, as the Wisdom of God in our midst. Then I will outline the notion of "deep incarnation" and bring the chapter to its conclusion by offering some thoughts on the meaning of Jesus Christ in the context of evolution. Chapter 6 will continue this exploration, focusing on the final transformation of all things in the risen Christ.

Creation in the Life and Ministry of Jesus

The living memory of Jesus was passed on orally in the liturgy, preaching, and life of the first Christian communities before finding written expression in the Gospels. In this living memory, Jesus is not only celebrated as messianic Son of God but also remembered as a great prophet and as an extraordinary teacher of wisdom. And like the long line of wisdom teachers of Israel, Jesus is remembered as someone who sees the natural world as the place of God.

As a wisdom teacher, Jesus speaks of God and God's reign in parables and proverbial sayings. He is a gifted parabler, communicating the deepest things of God in stories and images from the natural world and from the cultural world of human communities. His images come from the whole of life: the beauty of wildflowers, the growth of trees from tiny seeds, crops of grain, bread rising, a woman sweeping a floor looking for what was lost, children playing games, the relationship between a shepherd and the sheep, the birds of the air, foxes and their lairs, rain falling, and the generosity of a parent to a wayward child.

The parables reflect a close observation of and delight in the natural world as the place of God. They could arise only in a person who looks on creation with contemplative and loving eyes. As C. H. Dodd concludes in his classic study, the parables reveal that for Jesus there is an "inward affinity between the natural order and the spiritual order." Dodd argues that "the sense of the divineness of the natural order is the major premise of all the parables."[1] Jesus' parables of the reign of God are the products of one who sees creation as the gift of God and as the place of divine presence.

The memory of Jesus' prayer in the wilderness is a further witness that for him, as for other mystics in the Jewish and Christian traditions, the natural world is a place of encounter with the living God. His prayer in the desert and in the hills of Galilee points to the wilderness as the place where he found communion with the God he proclaimed. The Gospels recount Jesus' going out into the wilderness for forty days at the beginning of his ministry. There he experiences temptation and, we are told, "he was with the wild beasts" and "the angels ministered to him" (Mark 1:15). It seems that Jesus experiences the wilderness and its wild creatures as the place of divine communication. The Gospels tell us that during his ministry Jesus regularly goes into the wilderness to find God. Mark describes Jesus getting up early and going out to a deserted place to pray (Mark 1:35). Luke, in one of his many references to Jesus at prayer, tells of his going out to a mountain to pray and spending the night in prayer (Luke 6:12). As Jesus' passion approaches, the three Synoptic Gospels tell of his praying outdoors in the garden of Gethsemane, where he struggles in darkness and pain and entrusts his life and death to God.

The Gospel memory of Jesus' parables taken from nature and his prayer in the wilderness provides a context for interpreting Jesus' explicit sayings about God's compassion for nonhuman creation. In these well-known texts, Jesus teaches that God feeds and clothes each bird of the air and each lily of the field (Matt 6:28; Luke 12:27) and speaks of God's care for every individual sparrow that falls to the ground (Matt 10:29; Luke12:6). The focal point of these sayings is God's provident care for human beings. But the assumption made in them is that every sparrow that falls to the ground matters to God. There is no doubt that the Gospels present God's provident care for human beings as unique and special—"the hairs on your head are all counted" (Matt 10:30)—but they also present this compassion and provident care as involving *every single sparrow*.

Jesus sees God as the one who can be addressed in a familial and very human way as *Abba* (Mark 14:36). He clearly sees God as a God for human beings, a God attentive to us with love, a God who cherishes human beings and brings them liberation and hope.[2] But for Jesus this *Abba* is also the Creator God, the one who makes the sun rise and who sends rain upon the just and the unjust (Matt 5:45). The God of Jesus is a God who is radically a God for human beings but also a God for all creatures. When Jesus' words about wildflowers and sparrows are understood in the context of his other parables taken from nature and his practice of prayer in the wilderness, I think it can be said with confidence that Jesus looks on wildflowers and sparrows with loving eyes and sees them as both loved by God and revelatory of God.

The Early Christian Community Sees Jesus as the Wisdom of God

The experience of Jesus' resurrection radically transformed the battered and defeated followers of Jesus. In the process it led them to reflect on his meaning and identity. It convinced them that what was present with them in the life, death, and resurrection of Jesus was nothing less than God. They were well aware of the humanity of Jesus. They had lived through the events of Jesus' ministry and humiliating death. They now needed to find a way of telling the story of Jesus as a story that begins from God. They needed to be able to speak of God's self-giving to us in Jesus. They needed to find ways of speaking of Jesus as "God-with-us" (Matt 1:23).

Recent scholarship has shown that devotion to Christ as one with God arose very early in the life of the church, as early as the pre-Pauline Christian community centered in Jerusalem.[3] In Paul's own writings it is simply taken for granted. Paul also takes it for granted that the risen Christ has a cosmic role. In a remarkable text Paul writes: "Yet for us there is one God, the Father, from whom are all things and for whom we exist, and one Lord, Jesus Christ, through whom are all things and through whom we exist" (1 Cor 8:6). Clearly Paul sees "all things" in the universe as in some way having their existence through Christ, and he sees Christ as involved not only with the origins of things but with their final transformation also. He sees the whole of creation as finding redemption and final liberation in Christ (Rom 8:21).

How does this cosmic view of the risen Christ arise? It seems that one of the contributing factors was the already existing theology of the Wisdom of God. In the biblical wisdom literature, God's self-communication is beautifully personified in female terms as the *Wisdom Woman* (ḥokmâ in Hebrew, *sophia* in Greek). In these wisdom writings, the Wisdom Woman is understood not as a second God alongside the God of the covenant, but as a way of talking about the presence and action of the one God of Israel.

There are two central characteristics of the Wisdom Woman. First, *she is intimately involved with the whole of creation.* She is pictured as with God in creation, a co-creator with God, a companion with God delighting in all God's creatures (Prov 8:22-31; Sir 24:3-7; Wis 7:25-8:1). Wisdom is a "tree of life" (Prov 3:18). It is by her that God founds the earth, establishes the heavens, breaks open the deep, and enables the clouds to drop down their dew as refreshing, life-giving rain (Prov 3:19-20). Second, *she comes to dwell in our midst.* She makes her home with us, sets her table, prepares her great banquet, and invites the poor and needy to come to eat and drink of what she has prepared (Prov 9:1-6; Sir 24:8-22). Wisdom is both the one in whom all things are created and the one who has now come to dwell among us.

While Jewish believers could see God's gift of the Law (*Torah*) as the Wisdom of God who has made her home among us (Sir 24:23), early Christian believers could identify Jesus as the Wisdom of God in our midst. Paul insists, against all competing human claims to wisdom, that the Wisdom of God is found revealed in Christ crucified (1 Cor 1:24, 30). He argues forcefully that God's Wisdom is revealed precisely in what seems to be the utter foolishness and powerlessness of the cross. Matthew sees Jesus as the Wisdom of God in our midst. It is Jesus who does the healing and liberating deeds of Wisdom (Matt 11:20) and who, as Wisdom comes to make her home with us, cries out: "Come to me all you that are weary and are carrying heavy burdens, and I will give you rest" (Matt 11:28). In the Gospel of John, Jesus-Wisdom is proclaimed as the Word made flesh (John 1:1-18) and is presented as the one who invites the poor and needy to his table and gives himself to them as the Bread of Life (John 6).

Throughout the New Testament there are texts that may be remnants of early Christian hymns, which sing of Jesus in terms that echo the wisdom tradition. In the short hymn in the opening of Hebrews, for example, Christ is presented, like Wisdom, as the one through whom God creates all things (Heb 1:2). We read that Christ is "the reflection of God's glory and the exact imprint of God's very being, and he sustains all things by his powerful word" (1:3). The description of the risen Christ, as the "reflection" and "imprint" of God and the one who "sustains" all things, echoes the Wisdom of Solomon, where it is said of *Sophia* that she is "the image of God" (7:26) and that "she reaches mightily from one end of the earth to the other, and she orders all things well" (8:1).

In each of these hymns, the words "all things" form a constant refrain. The repeated use of this expression points insistently to the cosmic meaning of Christ. A second example of a Wisdom-type hymn to the risen Christ is found in the opening chapter of John's

Gospel. Here Jesus is again understood in categories and in language taken from the Wisdom literature,[4] but he is described as the Word of God rather than the Wisdom of God:

> In the beginning was the Word, and the Word was with God, and the Word was God. He was in the beginning with God. All things came into being through him, and without him not one thing came into being. . . . He was in the world, and the world came into being through him; yet the world did not know him. . . . And the Word became flesh and lived among us. (John 1:1-14)

Jesus is celebrated as the Word made flesh. But we are being told that the story of this Word does not begin with the life of Jesus. The Word was with God in the beginning and had an active role in the creation of "all things." According to this hymn, everything that has ever come to be in the long history of creation exists only in and through the Word. In terms of what we know today, this would involve seeing this Word of God as the Word of the Big Bang, the primordial hydrogen, star formation, the Milky Way Galaxy, planet Earth, bacteria, clams, frogs, and chimpanzees. It is this endlessly *creative* Word that is made flesh in Jesus. What is further suggested is that the whole process of the creation of the universe is directed toward the Christ-event.

A third example of a cosmic hymn to the risen Christ modeled on Wisdom is found in Colossians:

> He is the image of the invisible God, the firstborn of all
>   creation;
> for in him all things in heaven and on earth were
>   created,
> things visible and invisible,
> whether thrones or dominions or rulers or powers—
> all things have been created through him and for him.
> He himself is before all things and in him all things hold
>   together.

He is the head of the body, the church;
he is the beginning, the firstborn from the dead, so that
he might come to have first place in everything.
For in him all the fullness of God was pleased to dwell,
and through him God was pleased to reconcile to
     himself all things,
whether on earth or in heaven,
by making peace through the blood of the cross.

                                  (Col 1:15-20)

Here the cosmic Christ is celebrated as both the *source* of creation and its *goal*: all things have been *created* in Christ and all things are *reconciled* in him. The words "all things" are repeated like a refrain. All things are created in Christ, who is the image (*icon*) of the invisible God. As in the wisdom literature *Sophia* is with God in creation and continually sustains all things, so in Colossians the risen Christ is the one in whom all things are created and in whom all things hold together. The Colossians hymn goes further, asserting that in Christ and Christ's cross God has reconciled all things to God's self. Everything in creation is created in Christ, sustained in him, and reconciled in him.

The universal role of Christ is driven home not just by the oft-repeated "all things," but also by the repeated explanation that this involves everything in what were seen as the two great cosmic realms of heaven and earth, and by the further insistence that it includes all the cosmic powers—"whether thrones or dominions or rulers or powers." In ancient cosmologies, these angelic beings were thought of as controlling the movements of the sun, the moon, and the stars. It seems that some at Colossae worshiped these cosmic powers, and the letter makes it clear that all cosmic forces are taken up by Christ and transformed in the power of the resurrection. Everything in the universe is to be transfigured in Christ-Wisdom, the *icon* of the invisible God.

In Colossians, Christ's death and resurrection are understood as the beginning of the transformation of the whole of creation. This same idea appears in Ephesians, where we are told that all things will be gathered up in the risen Christ (1:9-10, 20-23). In Revelation, we hear of "a new heaven and a new earth," and the risen Christ is proclaimed the *Alpha* and the *Omega*, the first and the last, the beginning and the end (Rev 22:13). In the yearly cycle of the liturgy, many Christians use these words from Revelation as they light the Easter candle from the new fire of the Easter Vigil. Then, illuminated by the light of the Easter candle, the symbol of the risen one, they listen to readings from scripture that tell the story of salvation beginning with the Genesis account of the creation of all things. Every Easter is a celebration of the whole of creation transformed in the light of the risen Christ. Far from being restricted to human beings, the Christ-event involves everything on Earth, from ants and beetles to pelicans and whales. It involves every part of the fourteen-billion-year story of our universe and of the 3.8-billion-year history of life on Earth.

In recent years, feminist theologians have led the way in recovering a theology of Jesus in terms of divine Wisdom, or *Sophia*. Some, like Elisabeth Schüssler Fiorenza have focused on Jesus as a child and prophet of *Sophia*.[5] Others, like Elizabeth Johnson, have developed a Christology of Jesus as the Wisdom of God. In this theology, Jesus is understood as revelatory of God symbolized as the female *Sophia*. This has the effect of breaking the stranglehold of androcentric thinking and points to the God-with-us in Jesus as beyond male and female, but inclusive of both.[6] In my view this opens up to a viable and life-giving wisdom Christology that is both feminist and ecological. Jesus the Wisdom of God can be seen as inclusive of both female and male, and of both human and nonhuman creation.[7]

Wisdom Christology, like Word-of-God Christology and Son-of-God Christology, involves a view of preexistence and incarnation. It proposes that what we meet in Jesus of Nazareth is someone who is God with us, truly of God and sent by God. But wisdom Christology contains a healthy reminder that what preexists is not the humanity of Jesus. It encourages a healthy negative theology about that which preexists in the divine life. It makes it clear that preexistent Wisdom is neither male nor female but transcends both. And it points to a divine Wisdom that finds expression not just in the human but in the whole of creation. This kind of wisdom theology is depicted in the beautiful mosaic in the Church of San Clemente in Rome, where the cross of Christ is the tree of life for all creatures.

Deep Incarnation

As theologians have attempted to articulate a Christian ecological theology, they have turned to the central idea of incarnation. At the heart of Christian faith is the affirmation that Jesus of Nazareth is the *Word made flesh* (John 1:14). What is meant by flesh in this affirmation is not only the fully human reality of Jesus but the whole of humanity embraced by God in the incarnation. As the great patristic theologians such as Irenaeus and Athanasius taught, in the Word made flesh God becomes human so that the whole of humanity might be healed, taken up into God and deified in God.

The meaning of the incarnation, of becoming flesh, is not restricted to humanity. The flesh that is embraced by God is not limited to the human. It includes the whole interconnected world of fleshly life and, in some way, includes the whole universe to which flesh is related and on which it depends. On this basis, Australian theologian Duncan Reid argues for an eco-Christology in which affirmations about God's embrace of humanity in the incarnation are always to be understood in the context of the wider claim that the Word has become flesh. Flesh points beyond the humanity of Jesus and beyond the human community embraced by God in the incarnation to the biological world of living creatures.[8] Flesh evokes the whole world of interrelated organisms. It suggests that in becoming flesh, God has embraced all creatures in the interconnected web of life. New Zealand theologian Neil Darragh comments on this line of thought: "To say that God became flesh is not only to say that God became human, but to say also that God became an Earth creature, that God became a sentient being, that God became a living being (in common with all other living beings), that God became a complex Earth unit of minerals and fluids, that God became an item in the carbon and nitrogen cycles."[9]

In Jesus of Nazareth, God becomes a vital part of an ecosystem and a part of the interconnected systems that support life on Earth. Danish theologian Niels Gregersen calls this the idea of *deep incarnation*. He argues that, in Christ, God enters into biological life in a new way and is now with evolving creation in a radically new way. In Christ, God is with all forms of life in their suffering limitation. The cross of Christ reveals God's identification with creation in all its complexity, struggle, and pain. Gregersen finds in the cross a microcosm of God's redemptive presence to all creatures that face suffering and death. He writes:

> In this context, the incarnation of God in Christ can be understood as a radical or "deep" incarnation, that is, an incarnation into the very tissue of biological existence, and system of nature. Understood this way, the death of Christ becomes an icon of God's redemptive co-suffering with all sentient life as well as with the victims of social competition. God bears the cost of evolution, the price involved in the hardship of natural selection.[10]

I believe that this concept of deep incarnation is faithful to the Christian tradition, which claims, with Paul, that the whole creation waits with "eager longing" for its liberation from "bondage to decay" and for "the freedom associated with the glory of the children of God" (Rom 8:19-23). It is congruent with the Colossians hymn referred to above, in which Christ is celebrated as the "icon of the invisible God," as the "firstborn of all creation," as the one in whom "all things in heaven and on earth were created," as the one in whom "all things hold together," and as the one through whom "God was pleased to reconcile to himself all things, whether on earth or in heaven, by making peace through the blood of the cross" (Col 1:15-20).

The concept of deep incarnation also reflects the insights of evolutionary biology concerning the interconnections of all living things in the one history of life on Earth. Biology does not allow us to see human flesh as an isolated reality. Human beings can only be understood as interrelated with the other life-forms of our planet and interconnected with the atmosphere, the land, and the seas that sustain life. A theology that takes biology seriously can see human beings only as part of the 3.8-billion-year history of life on Earth. Precisely because theology is committed to God as Creator, it must take biology seriously. A biologically informed theology cannot think of the human without taking into account our dependence on the creatures that have gone before us in evolutionary history and our ecological interdependence with the biological systems of the planet.

Today, in a world where countless forms of life have been destroyed and many more are under threat, we need a deeper appropriation of the meaning of *God-with-us* in Christ. We need to think of *God-with-us* in the sense of *God-with-all-living-things*. In the concept of deep incarnation, the Christ-event can be understood as God entering into the evolutionary history of life on Earth, embracing finite creaturely existence from within. In the Word made flesh, God is revealed at the heart of the human, and therefore at the heart of all life on Earth. The flesh of Jesus is part of the whole creaturely pattern of life on Earth. When the Word is made flesh, God embraces the long, interconnected history of life in all its complexity and diversity. The incarnation is God-with-us in the "very tissue" of biological life. If God is with us in Christ Jesus in the very tissue of biological life, this raises further questions about the theological connection between the event of Christ and evolutionary history.

Jesus Christ in an Evolutionary World

Karl Rahner has offered some important reflections on the compatibility of Christology with an evolutionary view of the world.[11]

He asks whether it is possible to find an inner relationship between the Christ-event and evolution. He seeks a coherent theology that is faithful to the Christian tradition's deepest insights into the meaning of Christ and that also respects the findings of evolutionary biology.

He begins from the fundamental *unity* of creation. This unity is found first in the fact that all things spring from the one Creator. Second, creatures are united now in one interrelated and inter-dependent evolving universe. Third, the whole of creation will reach its culmination by being taken up as one into God. Creation is united in its one origin, in its self-realization as one united world, and in its one future in God. This unity is grounded in God's purpose in creating a universe of creatures.

Rahner describes this purpose in his beautiful fundamental concept of divine *self-bestowal*. God creates a universe of creatures in order to give God's self to them in love. Self-bestowal is the meaning of the universe. We human beings have experienced this self-bestowal in the Christ-event and in the experience of the Spirit in grace. In the Word made flesh and the Spirit given in grace, God is revealed as a God of self-bestowing love. Creation is the addressee of divine self-bestowal. This self-bestowal is already at work in our world in God's creative presence to all things. It will reach its culmination only when the whole of created reality is transfigured in the power of the resurrection and taken up into God.

Rahner sees the incarnation as intrinsic to God's purpose in creation. While one school of theology has seen the incarnation primarily as a remedy for human sin, another associated with Franciscan theologians such as Raymond Lull and Duns Scotus sees the incarnation as always central to the divine plan in creating a universe of creatures. In this second school of theology, creation was *always* directed toward the Christ-event. God always had the incarnation in mind.[12] Rahner takes up this Franciscan theology and argues that the universe exists only because God was always going to give God's self to creation in love. This means that the incarnation is not something that comes about primarily because of sin—although in a sinful world it certainly is an event of forgiving grace. The incarnation was always at the center of the divine plan. For Rahner, creation and incarnation are two distinct parts of the one act of God's self-bestowal to the world. They are two distinct dimensions of one process of divine self-giving. They always belong together.[13]

With this conviction in mind, Rahner begins to develop an evolutionary approach to Christology by pointing to the transitions that occur in evolutionary history. There are times when something radically new emerges, when more comes from less. Key examples are when matter becomes life and when life comes to self-consciousness in human beings. Rahner insists that the emergence of the new comes about through natural processes that have their own integrity. It is the role of science to explain these processes at the empirical level. But he sees an important role for theology as well. Theology needs to account for these processes in terms of the creative act of God. This demands a new development. How can a theology of creation account for the emergence of the new?

In the traditional theology of creation, God was seen as holding all creatures in being and as enabling them to act. Rahner finds this theology, important and fundamental as it is, in need of development. In the light of what science tells us about an emergent universe, creation cannot be thought of as God simply sustaining things in existence. Theology needs to give an account of God's creative act in such a way that it is seen as enabling the universe to *become*. God's creative act must be of such a kind as to allow the new and the unpredictable to emerge. God, then, needs to be thought of as empowering the universe from within, in such a way as to enable genuine novelty to emerge. As I pointed out in the last chapter, Rahner calls this creation's capacity for *self-transcendence*. This is a capacity that the universe and its creatures have within themselves to become. It belongs to the creature, but it is not due to the creature. It springs from the immanent creative presence of God enabling the creature not only to exist but to become what is new. As I proposed in the last chapter, it comes from the Creator Spirit present to each and every entity of the universe.

In Rahner's central idea, God is seen as inspiring and enabling a great pattern of evolutionary emergence. In this pattern, matter transcends itself to become life; life transcends itself in self-conscious human beings; human beings transcend themselves in union with God through grace; and in Jesus of Nazareth the whole evolutionary process transcends itself radically into God.

From the perspective of Christian faith, the universe can be thought of as carried from the beginning toward a more conscious relationship to its Creator. In human beings, the material universe has become self-conscious. In humanity creation has come to personhood. As creation come to personhood, human beings stand before God's self-offering love in the Spirit. As part of the universe, they are invited into an interpersonal relationship with the Creator. They are part of the universe that can turn back to God in love, thanksgiving, and praise.

In Jesus of Nazareth, this movement of grace reaches a moment when one human being is wholly and irreversibly responsive to God's self-giving love. In Jesus, one of us, part of the one universe and its history, is so radically open to and identified with God, that we can rightly say that he *is* the Wisdom of God, the Son of God. Like us, Jesus is the product of biological evolution. Like us, he is made from stardust. Like us, Jesus is interrelated to all other creatures in one global community of Earth. In Jesus, the movement of self-transcendence that has been going on throughout evolutionary history reaches its irreversible climax. In Jesus' complete yes to God, there is a radical and unique self-transcendence of creation into God.[14]

From the side of creation, then, the event of Jesus Christ can be understood as the self-transcendence of the created universe into God. From the side of God, Jesus can be seen as God's self-communication to creation. In Jesus, we find both God's self-giving to the universe and the universe responding in radical creaturely acceptance. Because Jesus is both God's self-communication in our history and creation's radical yes to God, Rahner sees Jesus as the absolute Savior.

Jesus is the self-bestowal of God, but this divine self-bestowal occurs from within the evolutionary history of life on our planet. Evolutionary history thus becomes the place of divine revelation. It is embraced by God and taken up into God. In the incarnation within evolutionary history, and above all in the resurrection that is its fulfillment, there is a promise that the history of life is not meaningless and empty. This history can now be seen as occurring because God wants to give God's self to creatures in love. In the resurrection there is a promise that this evolutionary history and all the creatures that it brings forth are destined to be taken up into God and to find in God their healing and divinizing fulfillment.

In this chapter, I have attempted to describe ways in which the living memory of Jesus can be understood in relation to ecological commitment. The starting point was with Jesus himself, with the memory of Jesus as a wisdom teacher who found God in creation and who saw God as involved with every sparrow that falls to the ground. At a second level, the first Christians see Jesus risen as the Wisdom of God, as the one in whom all things are created and finally reconciled. At a third level of reflection, I turned to the contemporary idea of deep incarnation, the idea that in the Word made flesh, God has embraced the whole interconnected world of biological life. Finally, I reflected on Rahner's insight that Jesus can be understood as both the self-transcendence of the evolving universe into God and as God's self-communication to the universe.

As this has made clear, bringing together commitment to Jesus Christ and commitment to creation is not a novelty in the Christian tradition. It can be grounded at the levels of the living memory of Jesus and of the wisdom Christologies of the early church. At the same time, recent scientific insights into the evolution of life and the interconnectedness of all life on our planet have led theologians to discover new levels of theological connection between Jesus and ecology, in the concepts of deep incarnation and the self-transcendence of creation. Each level contributes to the conviction that the following of Jesus in the twenty-first century necessarily involves ecological commitment. This will be taken further in chapter 6 in a theology of the transformation of creation in Christ. Before then, it will be helpful to explore the relationship between the trinitarian God revealed in the Christ-event and creation.

5

The Diversity of Life and the Trinity

The Earth is a place of glorious, abundant, and exuberant life. The wildly differing species that inhabit our planet have emerged over the last six hundred thousand years. They have a common heritage that goes back much further, to the origins of bacterial life more than 3.5 billion years ago. They have evolved in relationship to each other, interconnected in delicate ecological systems. They are interdependent not only with each other but also with the Earth's atmosphere, seas, rivers, and lakes, and the land itself.

Human actions such as releasing greenhouse gases into the atmosphere, ruthless fishing practices, the dumping of industrial and urban waste, the destruction of river systems and uncontrolled clearing of land destroy beautiful and mysterious species of creatures forever. A great number of these are unknown and unnamed. It is likely that among the unknown species there are many that could contribute to human health and well-being. If present trends are allowed to continue, the Earth will become a far more sterile and dangerous place. Human life will be radically impoverished.

The task facing the human community is clear. We are called to save what can be saved of the diversity of life. This may be the single greatest challenge that humans have ever been called upon to face. It is a task that will require every bit of human intelligence, cooperation, generosity, and commitment. There are clearly established scientific, medical, economic, aesthetic, and cultural reasons that motivate a commitment to biodiversity.

For those who stand within the great monotheistic religious traditions, there is a more radical reason for commitment to biodiversity.

For them it has to do with God, with the Creator who breathes the breath of life into all living things (Gen 2:7; Job 34:12-15; Ps 104:29-30). Judaism, Islam, and Christianity all profess faith in the one God who creates the whole universe and all its creatures. Together they hold that this Creator holds all things in existence, finds all of creation good, and enables it to flourish in all its fertility and abundance (Gen 1:20-31). Creation is the work of God. It is something humans must honor if they are to honor God. In this context, to destroy habitats and bring about the extinction of species in an arbitrary way can only be seen as a terrible sin against the Creator.

Jews, Christians, and Muslims worship the same Creator God, the one God of Abraham and Sarah, the God of Moses, the God of Jesus, and the God of Muhammad. Conscious of what we hold in common, I will explore the specifically Christian view of God as Trinity. This will involve a discussion of the emergence of the idea of God as communion, the theology of *perichoresis*, and the contemporary retrieval of the Trinity as a liberating doctrine. I will attempt to show how these reflections open out into a fully ecological theology, in that the diversity of creatures can be seen as the self-expression of the Trinity and that the ecological relationships that characterize life on Earth can be understood as springing from the relational life of the Trinity.

God as Communion

Although the word "Trinity" was not used until the late second century, the religious experience of the first Christian communities was already trinitarian. In Jesus, they experienced the healing, liberating, saving presence of God. Using categories taken from their tradition, they understood him as the messianic Son of God, as the Wisdom of God, and as the Word of God. They saw him as coming from God, as sent by God, and as God-with-us.

They knew Jesus as the Spirit-filled one, as anointed by the Spirit, as the bearer of the long-awaited Spirit, and as the risen one who sends the Spirit upon his disciples. They experienced the Holy Spirit as the life-giving, energizing presence of God, as the one who had formed them into the church of Jesus Christ and who had been poured out upon each as the power of resurrection life, making them children of God and enabling them to address God as *Abba* (Rom 8:15).

From the beginning, the Christian community saw both Jesus and the Spirit as sent from the one who is the Source of All, the one whom Jesus called *Abba* (Gal 4:4-7). Word and Spirit come from the Source of All to bring salvation. The original Christian experience was an experience of God acting to save us, through Jesus and the Spirit. The focus was on God's saving action, on what theologians sometimes describe as the "economy" of salvation. For the first Christians, salvation was experienced in a trinitarian way—as coming to us from God through Jesus and the life-giving Spirit. The focus was not on the inner life of God, but on what God was doing for us in the Word made flesh and in the Spirit poured out.

Eventually, the Christian community was forced to address questions that touch on the inner life of God. If Jesus is the Word made flesh, is this Word to be understood as eternal and divine or simply as a creature? Is the Spirit poured out upon us the presence of God or some created intermediary? And if the Christian community proclaims Word and Spirit as divine, how does this sit with the biblical commitment to monotheism?

As it struggled with these questions, the Christian community's response was grounded in a conviction about God's fidelity. They were convinced that God's self-revelation in Jesus and the Spirit faithfully represents the truth of who God is. When public disputes arose in the Arian controversies of the fourth century over the eternity and divinity of the Word and Spirit, the Christian community articulated its conviction of the full divinity of the Word at the Council of Nicaea (325) and of the Spirit at the Council of Constantinople (381).

Basil and the Eastern Tradition

Athanasius (ca. 296-377), patriarch of Alexandria, is a vigorous defender of the divinity of Word and Spirit in the unity of being of the one God. His strongest arguments have to do with salvation. At the heart of his theology of salvation is the idea that human beings are deified in Christ—transformed by grace and enabled to participate in the life of God. Only if Christ is truly God can our humanity be understood as deified in Christ. And since it is the Holy Spirit who makes us partakers in the divine life, this Spirit who sanctifies and deifies us cannot be a creature but must be divine, sharing the one divine nature.

The further development of a theology of the Holy Spirit, and of the Trinity, in the second half of the fourth century was largely the work of three bishop-theologians of Cappadocia, part of modern Turkey. These three theological collaborators were Basil of Caesarea (ca. 330-379), his younger brother Gregory of Nyssa (ca. 330-395), and their friend Gregory of Nazianzus (330-389).

Basil's important work *On the Holy Spirit* probably appeared about 375. He tells us that the occasion for writing the treatise was the controversy that erupted when he used a particular form of the trinitarian prayer of praise, the doxology: "Glory be to the Father *with* the Son *together with* the Holy Ghost." What his opponents objected to, and what Basil defends, is the idea that the Son and the Holy Spirit are "with" the Father. This "with" communicates the idea of equality and mutuality.

While Basil sees Word and Spirit as both coming eternally from the one who is Source of All, he sees the three as with each other in a unity in which there is no subordinationism. They are with each other in profound communion. The unity of the divine being, of the one divine substance, is the unity of a communion (*koinōnia*) of radical equality and mutuality. Basil defends the use of the word "with" to describe this communion because it brings out two things, first, that the Persons are truly distinct and, second, that they are inseparably united in the deepest communion.

For Basil and the other Cappadocians, this radical communion does not diminish or obscure what is distinctive and proper to the three Persons. On the contrary, they develop a new, powerful way of speaking that brings out the distinctiveness and uniqueness of each trinitarian person. Up until this stage, there is no strong word for the person in Greek or Latin. The Greek word available is *prosōpon*—taken from the actor's mask. It points to a role one plays. Wanting to bring out something far deeper, the Cappadocians begin to use the word *hypostasis* (underlying reality) for the three Persons. This initiates an important shift in Western culture—as persons (human as well as divine), can now be understood as foundational, as primordial, as having ontological weight and therefore as possessing their own dignity.

This new concept of person is radically relational. The trinitarian Persons are always Persons-in-relationship. With the Cappadocian theology, God is understood as Persons-in-Communion. This theology puts persons and relationships as the origin and the goal of the created universe. Everything that exists springs from the divine communion and will find its fulfillment only in this communion. With theologians like Basil, the three are thought of as being with each other in a divine communion of complete mutuality, equality, and unity. God, then, is thought of not as a solitary individual but as the three in a dynamic communion in love. God is radically relational: God's being is being-in-mutual-relations.

Augustine and the Western Tradition

In the West, the theology of the Trinity is taken up and developed by Augustine (354-430) in his *De Trinitate*, a work animated by Augustine's passionate quest for God. He explores the mystery of the Trinity as a program for the spiritual life, a discovering of oneself in God and of God in oneself. This exploration begins from the scriptures and the history of salvation and then, in the second half of the work, turns inward to find God reflected in God's image—the human person. Augustine names but does not develop the image of the lover, the beloved, and the love between them. His favored image is based on the interiority of the human person. He finds God reflected in the action of the inner self (the *mens*), in which this inner self remembers itself, understands itself, and loves itself. Augustine's supreme image for the Trinity is the inner self remembering God, understanding God, and loving God.

The greatest theologian in the Western tradition is the Dominican friar Thomas Aquinas (1225-1274). He follows Augustine in taking his principal image for the Trinity from human interiority and brings this line of thought to a new metaphysical depth. He sees the two activities of the human mind, knowing and loving, as corresponding to the two trinitarian processions of the Word and the Spirit. God's being is a pure act that is simultaneously a knowing and a loving. God's being as self-expressive generates the Word, which then stands in relation to the One expressing the Word. The love that is breathed forth between these two constitutes a third in God, the Spirit, standing in a relation to the other two with all the fullness of personhood.

God is understood as a dynamic act of self-communication and freedom. In creation, this circular dynamism opens out to include creatures. The circle of divine life is an open circle in which all things are created in the Word and brought into unity by the Spirit. Aquinas's understanding of God takes a different form from that in the East, but it is just as radically relational. He insists that the distinct relations in God cannot be something extrinsic or "accidental." The relations are identical with the divine nature. Aquinas calls them "subsistent" relations because they belong to God's substance. The relations belong to God's very being. They are who God is.[1]

The theology of Richard of St. Victor (d. 1173) is closer to the communion theology of the East. Building on Augustine's image of the lover, the beloved, and the love they share, Richard reflects on the Trinity in the light of the experience of mutual friendship. He sees the experience of mutual love as the greatest good that can be found in this life. He argues that, based on this experience, it is plausible to suppose that this highest good of mutual love would be found in its most sublime form in the divine life. And of course, if mutual love that goes out from the self to the other (*caritas*) is found in God, then God must be interpersonal. The human experience of mutual love, when it is not closed in upon itself but open to more than two, can be seen as a pale reflection of the dynamic, mutual, and equal love of the Trinity.

Bonaventure (1221-1274), the great Franciscan contemporary of Aquinas, draws on the East for the idea of the dynamic fruitfulness of divine goodness. This notion of fruitfulness or "fecundity" connects his theology of creation with his theology of the Trinity. He sees the fecundity of creation pointing back to the dynamic, boundless fruitfulness of the Trinity. In the life of the Trinity, everything flows from the fecundity of the Source of All, whom Bonaventure calls the Fountain Fullness (*fontalis plenitudo*). He sees the eternal Word of Wisdom of God as the Exemplar, the image of Fountain Fullness. When God freely chooses to create, the fruitfulness of trinitarian life finds wonderful expression in the diversity of creatures. Each different kind of creature is a reflection and image of the eternal Word. In the spirit of Francis, Bonaventure sees each creature as a self-expression of the Trinity, an important idea to which I will return later in this chapter.

Perichoresis—Unity in Diversity

The idea of mutual indwelling is a central idea in the long history of the Christian theology of the Trinity. Its most obvious biblical foundation is in the Gospel of John. In chapter 14, Jesus states: "I am in my Father and the Father is in me" (John 14:10-11). After this, Jesus promises the disciples that the *Advocate Spirit* will abide with them, dwelling in them forever (14:15-17). Then he promises that *he himself* will be with them: "I am coming to you. . . . On that day you will know that I am in my Father, and you are in me, and I am in you" (14:18-20). Finally he promises that *the Father* will dwell in them: "Those who love me will keep my word, and my Father will love them and we will come to them and make our home with them" (14:23).

In the following chapter of the Gospel, Jesus speaks at length of the mutual indwelling between himself and disciples with the image of the vine and the branches: "Abide in me as I abide in you. Just as the branch cannot bear fruit by itself unless it abides in the vine, neither can you unless you abide in me" (15:4). Finally, in chapter 17, Jesus prays for the community of disciples that they may be a sign of divine mutual love to the world: "I ask not only on behalf of these, but also on behalf of those who will believe in me through their word, that they may all be one. As you, Father, are in me and I am in you, may they also be one in us, so that the world may believe that you have sent me" (17:21). In these texts from John's Gospel, mutual indwelling is presented as characterizing not only the divine life, but also the life of the community of disciples and their witness in the world.

This idea of being-in-one-another is fundamental to all thinking about the Trinity. On the one hand, it preserves the diversity and uniqueness of the Three against the tendency to collapse the Trinity into an undifferentiated unity, as if God merely appears in different ways in the history of salvation (modalism). On the other hand, it preserves the radical unity of the Trinity against any tendency to see God as three separate individuals, as three gods (tritheism). From its origins, the concept of being-in-one-another is thought of not as something that involves only the inner life of God, but rather as something that opens out, in the free divine decision that involves creation and redemption, to include a world of creatures. In the Spirit, the triune God embraces a world of creatures, enabling them, each in its own way, to share in the mutual interrelationships of the Three.

This being-in-one-another of the Trinity came to be called *perichoresis*, a word that was mediated to both Eastern and Western theology through the work of John Damascene (675-749). The idea behind the Greek word *perichoresis* is something like that of an encircling embrace. It suggests a being present to one another in radical intimacy—a mutual presence in love. It is close to, but distinct from, a word that means to dance around the other. The divine dance is, nevertheless, a beautiful image that brings out the dynamism of the divine relationships that sustain and nourish creation.

Perichoresis points to unity in diversity. It refers to a communion in which diversity and unity are not opposed but enable each other to exist. Perichoresis expresses the intimate presence of one divine Person to the others, the being-in-one-another in supreme distinctiveness and freedom. In this type of unity, the individual Person is enabled to flourish precisely by being in communion with the other. The very being of divine Persons is relational. Each exists only in relationship to the other. Each Person is present to the other in a joyous and dynamic union of shared life. The concept of perichoresis means that fullness of personhood in the divine life, and by implication also in human life, flourishes precisely by being in the most intimate communion.

At the heart of the idea of perichoresis is the idea of the *ecstatic* relations of the Persons. In common usage the word "ecstasy" can mean any kind of blissful experience. In its Greek origins, however, and in its theological meaning, *ek-stasis* points to the idea of going-out-from-the-self. The perichoretic relations of the Trinity suggest that to be a person is not to be simply self-contained but to be able to go out from the self in love to the other. It suggests that true personhood, whether divine or human, is characterized by being in relationship to the other.

Both Eastern and Western theologies of the Trinity lead to a view of God as essentially relational. Both teach that the diversity of creatures springs from the overflowing abundance of divine perichoresis. While the Eastern tradition rightly insists that in the Trinity, the Father is the Source of All, it also insists that the divine communion of the Trinity is "not the result of a process, but a primordial given."[2]

In the Western tradition, the Trinity is relational in essence and, with Bonaventure and other theologians, the concept of perichoresis is adopted in a Latin form.[3] In both traditions, the Persons of the Trinity exist only in relation to each other, only as interpersonal, only as in communion. In both, the diversity of creatures is seen as springing from the overflowing abundance of the divine communion. Greek Orthodox theologian John Zizioulas sums this up beautifully with the statement: "It is communion that makes things 'be'; nothing exists without it, not even God."[4]

The Trinity as a Liberating Doctrine

The end of the twentieth century and the beginning of the twenty-first have seen a revival of interest in trinitarian theology. It has been rediscovered as a practical doctrine, a doctrine that has to do with salvation, one that has liberating implications for an understanding of the human person as a being-in-relationships, of creation as springing from divine communion, and of the church as a living sign of this divine communion.

A defining characteristic of our times, one often associated with the idea of the "postmodern," is the insight that we need to affirm and accept difference. Unity without respect for difference quickly collapses into a totalitarian situation where one view or one interest dominates over others. Trinitarian theology affirms not only communion but also difference. It locates unity in difference at the heart of God. A trinitarian theology supports a relational view of reality, but it is a specific kind of relationality, one in which distinction and difference are enabled to flourish.

I will point briefly to comments from theologians of the Orthodox, Catholic, and Protestant traditions, indicating how they see trinitarian theology leading to a relational view of the human and of creation. Orthodox theology insists not only on the unity in diversity of the Trinity, but that this diversity belongs to the very being of God. As Vladimir Lossky says, in God "diversity is an absolute reality."[5] John Zizioulas sees trinitarian theology as providing a basis for understanding the person and reality itself as ecstatic. What a thing is, he says, "is not answered by pointing to the 'self-existent,' to a being as it is determined by its own boundaries, but to a being which in its *ekstasis* breaks through these boundaries in a movement of communion."[6] There can be no true being without communion.[7] Boris Bobrinskoy defines the human person, made in the divine image, as a *being of communion.* It is this person, as a being of communion, who is renewed in Christ and transformed from within by the Holy Spirit. In this transformation we and the universe we inhabit participate in God: "What is at stake is a deification that is both personal and cosmic, and which can be accounted for only in trinitarian categories."[8]

Catholic theologian Walter Kasper understands the unity of the divine nature as a "unity in love." The means that the final word about the nature of reality belongs not to "static substance" but to "being-from-another and being-for-another."[9] Catherine LaCugna, too, sees the doctrine of the Trinity as opening out into an understanding that relationships are at the very heart of reality, both divine and creaturely. She writes that "God's To-Be is To-Be-in-relationship, and God's being-in-relationship-to-us *is* what God is."[10] Elizabeth Johnson writes that the Trinity, as pure relationality, "epitomizes the connectedness of all that exists in the universe." It points to the dynamic relational life of God at work in the universe. It provides "a symbolic picture of totally shared life at the heart of the universe."[11]

Protestant theologian Jürgen Moltmann sees the Trinity as making space within the divine relational life for a creaturely world to emerge: "the trinitarian relationship between the Father, the Son and the Holy Spirit is so wide that the whole creation can find space, time and freedom in it."[12] Colin Gunton writes that "of both God and the world it must be said that they have their being in relation."[13] This means, he says, that to be personal is not primarily to be an individual center of consciousness, but "to be one whose being consists in relations of mutual constitution with other persons."[14]

More recently Graham Buxton has argued that "relationality is a critical—even essential—dimension of the divine imprint on creation." He sees perichoresis as not only a way of articulating the divine life of the Trinity, and not only as a way of thinking and speaking about the communion of Christians with each other and with the wider human community, but also as a "principle of cosmological unity."[15]

These different theologians from different traditions agree in arguing that if God's being is a communion of mutual love, then this has profound consequences for a view of human persons in relation to others. It offers a basis for a sustained critique of all patriarchal, dominating, and exploitative human relations in society at large and, above all, in the life of the church. They agree in proposing, too, that if the Creator's being is radically relational, then this suggests something about the nature of created reality. It suggests that reality is *ontologically* relational. The very *being* of things in our universe is relational being.

The Diversity of Creatures as the Self-Expression of the Trinity

We are still a very long way from knowing the number of different species on Earth. We have identified about 1.8 million species of animals. Scientific estimates of the total number of species vary greatly, but it is thought to be at least six to ten million, with some estimates much higher. Many of these creatures live in tropical rain forests, and one to two percent of the forests are being lost each year. Because of the loss of these forests, and the loss of other habitats, many species are being forced into extinction. This can only be an affront to a God who delights in creatures in all their diversity and specificity. This divine delight embraces all the species of birds, from the blue wren to the great albatross. It includes all the different kinds of hopping creatures we find in Australia, all the species of kangaroos, wallabies, pademelons, potoroos, bettongs, and bilbies. It includes all the diverse, sometimes beautiful and sometimes strange, creatures found in the ocean depths and the thousands of forms of bacterial life found in a handful of soil from a garden.

This abundance of life springs ultimately from the abundance of the divine communion. It expresses the ecstatic nature of the divine life. The divine Persons are ecstatic not only in their being-with-each-other, but in choosing to be with a world of creatures. This idea was beautifully developed by Bonaventure. I have already described how he was fascinated by the fecundity of God. He saw this fecundity expressed first of all in the divine life as the one he called the Fountain Fullness (*fontalis plenitudo*) eternally brings forth the Word and the Spirit. In the fecundity of the generation of the Word, he saw already contained the possibility of the endless variety of creatures. In God's creative act, this endless fecundity of trinitarian life explodes forth into the diversity of creatures.

Bonaventure tells us that God creates the perceptible world "as a means of self-revelation." Each creature represents the divine Wisdom. Each is a work of art produced by Wisdom. Like a mirror, each reflects the divine artist. In each there is an imprint (*vestigium*) of the Trinity. Bonaventure also used the image of the book: the universe is "like a book reflecting, representing and describing its Maker, the Trinity."[16] Another image he uses is taken from the stained-glass windows of medieval churches. As the one stream of light breaks up into different colors as it flows through a stained-glass window, so the Creator is reflected in the different creatures we see around us. Each and every creature reflects a different aspect of the Creator.[17] The exuberance of creation represents the infinite fecundity of God.

Thomas Aquinas writes something similar:

The distinction and multitude of things come from the intention of the first agent, who is God. For God brought many things into being in order that his goodness might be communicated to creatures and represented in them; and because this goodness could not be adequately represented by one creature alone, God produced many and diverse creatures, so that what was wanting to one in the representation of divine goodness might be supplied by another. For goodness which in God is simple and uniform, in creatures is manifold and diverse. Hence the whole universe together participates in the divine goodness more perfectly, and represents it better than any single creature whatever.[18]

No one creature, not even the human, can image God by itself. Only the diversity of life—huge soaring trees, the community of ants, the flashing colors of the parrot, the beauty of a wildflower along with the human—can give expression to the radical diversity and otherness of the trinitarian God. The diverse species we find on Earth can be seen as sacraments of God. They express and represent the one who fills all things and holds all things in existence. Such a view challenges the ruthless human destruction of species and their habitats in the modern era.

Diversity receives its most radical validation from a God who encompasses difference in communion. As Belden Lane has said, we are summoned to celebrate not only a world that thrives on dissimilarity and difference but also a God who thrives on diversity. This view of God puts an ethical demand upon us: "the doctrine of the Trinity demands an ethical practice that honors difference within the lively exchange of a loving community."[19] Again, this calls us beyond the human comfort zone to an appreciation of nature in all of its reality, including not only what we find ourselves responding to as beautiful but also what at first seems alien and mysterious. Even what is alien can lead us into the radical mystery of love that surrounds us and that finds expression in the diversity of creation.

Relational Universe—Relational God

In the previous section, I suggested that the diversity of creatures gives expression to the fecundity and abundance of the divine life.

But an ecological view sees organisms and species not in isolation but as part of an interrelated world. In this section I will propose that the ecological relationships that characterize life on Earth are part of a wider pattern of relationships in nature and that these relationships can be understood as grounded in the trinitarian relations of mutual love.

Relationships between entities characterize every stage of the emergence of our universe. New patterns of organization give rise to new entities. Science points to patterns of emergent relationships everywhere. Everything in our universe is made of fundamental particles such as hydrogen, oxygen, and carbon. Collections of atoms make up molecules. These make up the chromosomes that carry the genetic code. They in turn are contained within the nucleus of a cell, the basic building block of life. While some organisms are single-celled, a human being is made up of about 50 trillion cells specialized to perform an enormous variety of tasks.

Emergence is a central characteristic of our universe. It appears in the particles formed in the first second of the Big Bang, in the hydrogen nuclei formed in the first few minutes, in the stars that synthesize further elements, in the DNA molecule, in the first cells that had a nucleus, in multicellular creatures, and in human brains. At every stage in this process, something that is genuinely new occurs. Atoms, stars, bacteria, eukaryotes, multi-cellular organisms, mammals, and human brains are emergent phenomena. Each of these depends on what goes before, but each represents something new. Without the patient unfolding of things in time, nothing at all could ever happen. The understanding of ourselves and other species as emergent creatures who evolve over time within an evolving universe demands a different view of reality from anything that was available to Plato, Aquinas, or Newton.

Entities emerge in our universe in patterns of interrelationship. Things are constituted by relationships. Arthur Peacocke has long pointed out that the natural sciences give us a picture of the world as a complex hierarchy, in which there is a series of levels of organization of matter in which each member in the series is a *whole* constituted of *parts* that precede it in the series.[20] When science studies a hydrogen atom, a galaxy, a cell, or the most complex thing we know, the human brain, it finds patterns of emergent relationships. New relationships between components and with the wider environment produce a richness that is not possessed by the components apart from these relationships.

A carbon atom is part of a molecule, which forms part of a cell, which belongs to an organ, which is part of my body. I am part of a family, a human society, and a community of interrelated living creatures on Earth. The Earth community depends on and is interrelated with the sun, the Milky Way Galaxy, and the whole universe. Entities are constituted from components yet not reducible to them. Cosmologist William Stoeger insists that it is a *universal* feature of the world revealed by the natural and social sciences that entities are constituted by relationships.[21] At every level, from fundamental particles to atoms, molecules, cells, and the brain itself, one level of reality is nested upon another. At every level, something new emerges with its own distinct properties.

The theological insight that God's being is relational can provide a basis for a vision of the fundamental reality of the universe as relational. While science tells us that each creature exists in a nested pattern of constitutive relations, theology grounds this in the trinitarian relationships of mutual love. Trinitarian theologians argue that if the Creator's being is radically relational, then this suggests something about the nature of created reality itself. It suggests a relational ontology. It suggests that the very *being* of things is relational. To use John Zizioulas's phrase once again, "It is communion that makes things 'be': nothing exists without it, not even God."[22]

What is proposed in all of this is a worldview in which not only human persons but also all other creatures, in their highly differentiated ways, are seen as radically interrelational and interdependent. And this world of interrelating entities can be thought of as emerging from within the dynamic relations of the trinitarian God. The interrelatedness that ecologists find in the biosphere on Earth and the interrelatedness that science discovers at all levels from quantum physics to cosmology are all sustained at every moment by a God who is Persons-in-communion. Our interrelated universe, with all its diverse creatures, emerges from the embrace of the divine communion in love. This gives unthinkable depth to the importance of ecological interrelationships.

6

The Final Transformation of All Things

Christianity is a religion of promise and hope. It is directed toward a future in God. The way in which this future is envisaged matters a great deal for an ecological theology. If Christianity is understood to be about leaving this world for a heavenly world, if we are only in this world for a short time before abandoning it for another, more spiritual one, then this world is devalued. It is merely a step along the way to something that is our ultimate goal. Some Christians think this way, and as a result, even when they value non-human creation as a gift of God, it has no final meaning. It is to be left behind on the spiritual journey to a better world.

This view of things is a dangerous one. It relativizes and demeans what we do in this life. When Christian faith is understood in this way, it is rightly subject to the Marxist critique that religion functions as a soothing and dulling "opium." It offers only "pie in the sky" and acts as a disincentive to active involvement in the struggle for a just world. In ecological terms, this view of Christian hope suggests that it is not a matter of final importance that we are polluting the land, the seas, and the atmosphere, destroying forests, causing climate change, and bringing extinction to uncounted species.

Although this understanding of the Christian promise may be widespread, it does not represent what is central to Christian faith. This faith proclaims a God who embraces *flesh* in the incarnation and who promises in the resurrection of Christ a bodily future in God for human beings and, in some way, for all things. In this chapter I explore what Christianity can say about the future of the universe and its creatures. I begin with two important Christian thinkers who insist that this material world we inhabit will be transformed in Christ and will have a future in God: Pierre Teilhard de Chardin and Karl Rahner. Then I take up an issue that they do not address, the place of nonhuman forms of life in this future of all things in God.

Christ the Omega: Pierre Teilhard de Chardin (1881-1955)

Pierre Teilhard de Chardin was born in the Auvergne region of France, and his life was shaped by his youthful passion for the rocks and fossils of the region. From an early age he found meaning in Ignatian spirituality, with its focus on the centrality of following Jesus and its commitment to finding God in all things. After joining the Jesuits and completing the normal courses of philosophy and theology, Teilhard studied paleontology at the Museum of Natural History in Paris. While his scientific work is important on its own terms, Teilhard is remembered for his attempt to build a vision that holds together the long reaches of evolutionary history and Christian faith in Jesus Christ.

This was dangerous territory in the Catholic Church of the early twentieth century. Church authorities, caught up in the aftermath of the "Modernist" crisis, had reservations about aspects of Teilhard's evolutionary thought, particularly its relation to the biblical accounts of creation. The result was that Teilhard was not allowed to publish his works during his lifetime and spent much of his professional life working in China, well away from France, his intellectual home. By the 1950s, when his books began to appear, the renewal of biblical scholarship and the contributions made by Teilhard and other thinkers had created a new, if still cautious, openness within the Catholic Church to evolution.[1]

During World War I, Teilhard volunteered to serve as a stretcher bearer, and in the trenches he began to develop the unified vision that he would spend his life articulating. This vision looks back over the long history of evolution, seeing the material universe giving rise to organic life, and organic life giving rise to human life. It looks forward, predicting a new stage of cosmic evolution, in which human beings will come to a new unity of consciousness. Teilhard sees this as a unity in love that, as a Christian, he understands as centered in Christ. Building on texts in Romans, Colossians, Ephesians, and John's Gospel, Teilhard thinks of the risen Christ as the "cosmic Christ." He sees the risen Christ as the Omega of evolution, the goal and fulfillment of the whole process. This Omega already exists and operates at the heart of the universe. Christ the Omega radiates the love that empowers the process of the unfolding of the universe. Teilhard sees the risen Christ as the Prime Mover of evolution, the one who actuates the energies of the universe. Christ the Omega draws the universe to its future in God and already empowers the whole process of evolutionary emergence from within.[2]

Teilhard's most influential books are *The Divine Milieu* and *The Human Phenomenon*. He completed work on *The Divine Milieu* in China in 1927. The word "milieu" is used to express the presence and action of God at every level of created reality. God is both the center that transforms all things and the environment in which this occurs. Teilhard argues that, through the incarnation and the resurrection, it is now the risen Christ who is present to all things. He writes that because of the incarnation, God's universal presence "has transformed itself for us into *the omnipresence of christification*."[3] As Ursula King says, the idea of the "divine milieu" captures "the universal influence of Christ through God's incarnation in the world, in its matter, life and energy."[4] *The Divine Milieu* is an extended reflection on the interior life. Teilhard structures the book around what he calls human *activities* and *passivities*, showing that in both we are taken up into God and divinized. God is present in both our creativity and in our suffering as the divine milieu, molding and transforming us into the whole Christ. Everything we do, and everything we endure with faith and love, including every diminishment and death itself, has enduring meaning before God.

In *The Human Phenomenon,* completed in 1940, Teilhard traces the great movement of evolution from the atom to the molecule, from the molecule to the cell, from the cell to the immense variety of living things, and from the diversity of life to the human. He traces this as a movement of increasing *complexity*. As the universe expands, it also grows in complexity. This increase in complexity is accompanied by an increase in *interiorization,* in the capacity for consciousness. Teilhard sees this trend toward increasing complexity, for which he finds evidence in evolutionary history, as a universal law. He calls it the law of complexity-consciousness.[5]

Teilhard's argument is that once this law has been established on the basis of the empirical study of the history of evolution, it is appropriate to project this movement forward into the future. He is convinced that the future increase in complexity will occur at the level of the interaction of human minds and in the development of human culture. Because the Greek word *nous* refers to the mind, Teilhard names the evolution that occurs in the social interactions between human beings the *noosphere.* He suggests that we can distinguish three main spheres in the emergence of the universe: the sphere of matter (the geosphere), the sphere of life (the biosphere), and the sphere of mind (the noosphere). He sees the future of evolution to be with the noosphere. Teilhard says that with the noosphere, the Earth "gets a new skin" and "finds its soul."[6]

In this vision, the evolution of the world will culminate in a transformation brought about by the power of love. Teilhard makes it clear, particularly in the epilogue to his book, that he sees this in terms of Christ. As Christopher Mooney has pointed out, there are really three levels of argument in Teilhard's work.[7] At the level of *science*, Teilhard argues that, based on the evolution of complexity and consciousness, the human community can cross a new threshold to a single collectivity of consciousness that he calls the Omega Point. Second, at the level of *philosophy*, progress toward higher forms of interpersonal communion demands a divine Center, an Omega, radiating the love that empowers the process. Finally, at the level of *theology*, Teilhard draws on Christian revelation and sees the risen Christ as the true Omega of evolution. The becoming of the universe, *cosmogenesis*, is really a being transformed into Christ, a *Christogenesis*. Christ radiates the energy that leads the universe to its culmination in God.

Teilhard has been criticized by some scientists who do not agree with his notion of progress in evolution and by others who find his thought an unacceptable mixture of science and religious faith. He has been criticized by theologians who find fault with his optimism, with what they see as an inadequate view of sin and with his failure to deal with the dark side of evolution. From the perspective of the twenty-first century, it is obvious that Teilhard did not foresee, and his work does not reflect, the ecological crisis.

Yet his radical commitment to this world, to matter, has an important word to speak to an age struggling toward an ecological view of reality. Teilhard's vision has inspired many Christians, and there are signs that it will be important in a new era.[8] Theologians like Karl Rahner have responded to the challenge of his work, seeking to make more clear the theological connections between faith in Jesus Christ and the future of the material universe.[9]

The Transformation of the Universe:
Karl Rahner (1904-1984)

Karl Rahner, like Teilhard, was a Jesuit priest. He was also a German theologian, a student of Thomas Aquinas who read Aquinas and the whole Christian tradition from a perspective influenced by post-Enlightenment philosophy, science, and contemporary experience. As a theological expert, he became an important influence on the work of the Second Vatican Council. After the council, his deeply thoughtful contributions on an astonishing variety of topics marked him as one of the great theologians of the twentieth century. I am convinced that his contributions on the future of the material universe form a solid basis on which to build an ecological theology of the future.[10]

Resurrection as the Beginning of Transformation
of the Universe

Rahner takes up issues raised by Teilhard from his own particular perspective. While his work is certainly informed by science, Rahner insists that he writes not as a scientist but simply as a theologian. In particular, his begins from the resurrection of Jesus, which he sees as a transforming event in the history of the universe. He draws on the Eastern Christian tradition, which has always understood the incarnation and with it Christ's death and resurrection as *transforming* reality forever. The focus is not on a forensic view of redemption, on Christ making up for human sin in legal terms, but on God embracing humanity and the world so that they are taken into God and deified.

Following this line of thought, Rahner sees the resurrection as a change at the deepest level of things in the universe. He calls this an ontological change, a change at the level of being. The resurrection is not to be seen simply as something that concerns what happens to the person of Jesus beyond death. It is an event in which part of this world (the human, bodily reality of Jesus) is taken up into God. Rahner speaks of the resurrection as the beginning of the divinization of the world itself.[11]

He sees the death and resurrection of Jesus as two distinct sides of the one event. In death, Jesus freely hands his whole bodily existence into the mystery of a loving God. In the resurrection, God adopts creaturely reality as God's own reality.[12] Jesus, in his humanity and as part of a creaturely world, is forever taken into God. God's self-bestowal to the world in the incarnation reaches its culmination in the resurrection, when God divinizes and transfigures the creaturely reality of Jesus.

This means that the resurrection of Jesus is an event for the whole of creation. Rahner sees God as creating a universe of creatures in order to give God's self in love to creatures. The very meaning of creation is God's self-bestowal in love to creatures and the resurrection is central in this self-bestowal. The self-giving of the incarnation culminates in the resurrection as the beginning of the transformation of reality from within. What has occurred in Jesus, as part of the physical, biological, and human world, is *ontologically* "the embryonically final beginning of the glorification and divinization of the whole of reality."[13]

As an aside, it is important to note that Rahner's strong claim that the resurrection of Jesus has meaning for the universe needs to be understood in a way that acknowledges the possibility that personal beings may exist on other planets. Rahner explicitly allows that such extraterrestrials may exist and that if they do, they may have their own history of salvation. He holds that it "cannot be proved that a multiple incarnation in different histories of salvation is absolutely unthinkable."[14] This means that when Rahner claims that the resurrection has meaning for the whole universe, this is to be understood in such a way that it does not rule out the possibility that such events may also occur in the histories of extraterrestrial communities.

Rahner's central claim is that the resurrection that occurred in Jesus is an objective change in the world of creatures. It is "the beginning of the transformation of the world as an ontologically interconnected occurrence."[15] In the resurrection of Jesus, the final destiny of the world is decided, and this future is already at work in the universe. Rahner sees Jesus as "pledge and beginning of the perfect fulfillment of the world." He is the "representative of the new cosmos." As the risen one, he is freed from "the limiting individuality of the unglorified body" and is able to be present to creation precisely as the risen one and as the power of resurrection life. Rahner suggests that his final glorious return will be "the disclosure of this relation to world attained by Jesus in his resurrection."[16]

Rahner sees the created humanity of Jesus, taken up into God in the resurrection, as forever that which unites the created universe and God. Jesus is always and everywhere the way to God: "This created human nature is the indispensable and permanent gateway through which everything created must pass if it is to find the perfection of its eternal validity before God." Jesus is always "the gate and the door, the Alpha and the Omega."[17]

He is forever the openness of created reality to God. In this theological vision, God's grace and our response to this are forever mediated through the risen Christ. The human reality of Jesus continues to be for eternity the enduring reality of the Word of God. All our acts of worship are taken up into God through the Word made flesh.

The created humanity of Jesus has eternal significance for the eternal life of human beings in God and for the final transformation of the whole of creation.

The Future as Mystery as well as Promise

While Rahner insists on the promise of a transformed creation, he insists just as strongly that we do not know what this will be like. God and God's future are beyond our limited human comprehension and imagination. The God of the future radically transcends the concepts and words that come from our experience of creaturely reality. God is always *incomprehensible mystery*. God is the future coming toward us precisely as what is beyond comprehension and imagination. We cannot picture this future in any coherent way. Because our future and that of the universe are a future in God, they participate in the incomprehensibility of God.

To think we could picture this final and definitive state "would be still more absurd than to suppose that the caterpillar could imagine what it would be like to be a butterfly." What we know, on the basis of the promise of God given in the resurrection, is that we will be brought to our fulfillment by being taken into the unfathomable loving mystery of God—and, Rahner says, "that is enough."[18] Rahner points out that what really matters is the promise of God, which can sustain us even in the darkness and unknowing of death. But, of course, a number of questions come to mind at this point. More can be said, and is said even by Rahner. However, I believe Rahner is right to insist that it must be said tentatively, with respect for the limits of what we know about our future in God.

Taking up a phrase usually associated with Nicholas of Cusa (1401-1464), Rahner speaks of a central task of Christian theology as guarding the *docta ignorantia futuri* (the "learned unknowing" of the future). With this expression, he insists that the critical role of theology is *to resist closure* with regard to the future. Theology's task is to keep open the question of the future, to recognize what we do not know.[19] I believe that this humble stance, involving radical trust in God's promise, on the one hand, and a clear recognition of what we do not know, on the other, has a new importance at the beginning of the twenty-first century. Not only does it offer an alternative to those who would dismiss all talk of a future in God as hopelessly mythological; it also offers an important corrective in a context where some influential groups of fundamentalist Christians misread biblical texts such as Revelation and make extravagant claims to detailed knowledge of the future.

Rahner insists on the importance of recognizing the *figurative* nature of the biblical texts that speak about the future. The great biblical images do not give us any kind of detailed description, but point to what is beyond imagination—the future of the universe and its creatures taken up into God. We know about this future on the basis of what we already experience, the God we experience in Jesus and in the Spirit.[20] Our hope in the future is based on the experience we already have of God's self-bestowing love.

Rahner insists that the promise of God involves the whole embodied person and the material universe. Those who die in God are not to be thought of as taken away from the body or from creation. They remain united with the reality and the events of the world. The second coming of Christ is not something that will be enacted on the stage of an unchanged world. Rather, the second coming will take place at the moment of the transformation of the world into the reality that Christ already possesses. Then, Rahner says, it will be seen that "the world as a whole flows into his Resurrection and into the transfiguration of his body." Christ then, "will be revealed to all reality and, within it, to every one of its parts in its own way, as the innermost secret of all the world and of all history."[21]

The Future of This Universe

In an article exploring the notion of "the new earth," Rahner faces up to the question put by Marxism: How seriously do Christians take the world of justice, peace, and integrity that they are trying to achieve?[22] Do they consider that it will be part of God's future, or is it something that will simply be done away with? Rahner's response is that the world we try to build has enduring significance. The coming reign of God will be the deed of God, but it will occur in and through creaturely history.

In Rahner's theological vision, God's action in the final transformation of the universe will occur, as elsewhere in God's dealings with creation, as the *self*-transcendence of creaturely history. Our history will endure, but it will be radically transformed. The history that we construct, with all our acts of creativity and love, is not lost but "passes into the definitive consummation of God."[23] The human effort to build a world of justice and ecological integrity has final meaning. It will be taken up and transformed in Christ.

Rahner sees the universe as sustained from the beginning by the creative impulse that enables the universe to transcend itself. This is the impetus of God's self-bestowal. The original creative impulse already contained the future incarnation of the Word. God always intended to embrace the material world in the incarnation and to bring it to its fulfillment in Christ. Matter is not something to be cast aside as a transitory stage in the journey of the spirit. The material world will be transformed in God. It has been carried from the beginning by God's self-bestowing love. Rahner speaks of this self-bestowal in love as "the most immanent element in every creature." Therefore he can say: "It is not mere pious lyricism when Dante regards even the sun and the other planets as being moved by that love which is God himself as he who bestows himself."[24] The innermost principle of the movement of the galaxies and their stars, the innermost principle of the expanding and evolving universe, is God present in self-bestowing love.

In a meditation on the Ascension, Rahner points to the work of the Spirit, the Holy *Pneuma* of God, as the resurrection power of God at work in the ferment of creation:

And already for this world as a whole, the process of fermentation has already commenced which will bring it to this momentous conclusion. It is already filled with the forces of the indescribable transformation. And this inner dynamism in

it is called, as Paul boldly confirms for us in speaking of the resurrection of the flesh, the holy *Pneuma* of God. It is a free
grace. It is not the sort of entity which the world could lay
claim to as something proper to itself, something belonging to
it autonomously and as of right. But it is the true, the ultimate
perfection of the world in all its power, which brooded and
hovered over the primordial chaos, and which will preserve all
things and perfect all things which were and are. And this
power of all powers, this meaning which is the ultimate meaning of all meanings, is now present at the very heart and centre
of all reality including material reality, and has already, in the
glorified Son, brought the beginning for the world tri-
umphantly to its final goal of perfection.[25]

Because the Holy Spirit at work in the material universe, because
of the Word made flesh, and because of the resurrection, Christians
cannot but be committed to matter.

Rahner sees Christians as "the most sublime of materialists." We
cannot think of our fulfillment without thinking of the fulfillment
of the material universe. We cannot conceive of the risen Christ
except as the Word of God existing forever in the state of material
incarnation. This means that "as materialists we are more crassly
materialist than those who call themselves so." We recognize that
matter will last forever and be glorified forever, but we also know it
will undergo a radical transformation, "the depths of which we can
only sense with fear and trembling in that process which we experience as our death."[26] Because of the incarnation and the resurrection, Christian theology is firmly committed to the body, to matter,
and to the universe. We cannot think of a future for ourselves in
God without thinking of the future of all God's creatures.

The Redemption of Individual Creatures in Christ

In my view, Rahner's theology of the transformation of all things
in Christ succeeds in bringing the material universe to the center of

Christian eschatology. But it raises further questions. One of them concerns the way such a Christian vision of the future relates to the predictions of scientific cosmology, which at present involve the universe endlessly expanding and cooling in bleak dissipation. This is an important issue in the current science–theology dialogue, but not one I can address here.[27] A second issue, which I will address because it is central for ecological theology, concerns the future of nonhuman living creatures in God.

While I am proposing that the insights of Teilhard and Rahner can be foundational for an ecological theology of the fulfillment of creation, they are not yet genuinely ecological. While both theologians, in their different ways, are fascinated by matter and its relationship to God, and while both acknowledge the evolutionary movement from matter to life to mind, neither focuses on other *living* creatures in relation to God. They tend to bypass biological life in their reflections on the future of the universe in God.

They do not respond directly to the question of the future of individual nonhuman organisms: Are these creatures in any way redeemed by the love of God poured out in Christ? Do individual creatures share eternally in the life of God? Jay McDaniel has posed this question by reflecting on the successful evolutionary strategy of some pelicans, which involves hatching an extra disposable chicken as an insurance against the loss of the primary chick. These "backup" chicks are often abandoned. McDaniel asks whether we may hope that such abandoned chicks will find their fulfillment and redemption in some kind of "pelican heaven."[28]

In attempting some response to this question, I think it is important to begin by saying once again with Rahner that we have no detailed information about the future of ourselves or any other creatures in God. What we have from the Christian tradition is the resurrection: a promise that we are held in the faithful love of God, which is stronger than death; a promise that we along with all things will be transformed in Christ. We also have the important insight from science that we human beings are deeply interconnected with all the living things on Earth. In the light of these convictions, it is the task of theology to attempt to articulate a plausible construct of final fulfillment. Such constructs are necessarily tentative and limited, dealing as they do with a future that involves the incomprehensible mystery of God.

The tentative proposal offered here draws upon the trinitarian theology of God as communion, on the ancient concept of the communion of saints and on the liturgical theology of memory (*anamnesis*). It starts from the assumption that the promise of the gospel involves a personal, bodily participation in resurrection life for human beings. Even though this issue raises questions for many people today, I will not focus on the future of humans. My focus will be directly on nonhuman creatures: How can we begin to think about an individual sparrow, salmon, or wallaby in relation to the future of creation in God? I will address this question in five steps, the first four of which are affirmations, while the last is simply an open question.

1. Every sparrow is known and loved by God. In the Gospels, Jesus speaks of God as involved with every sparrow that falls to the ground (Matt 10:29; Luke 12:6). While this saying is focused on God's provident care for human beings, it assumes that God's provident care also involves *every single sparrow*. In chapter 2, I argued that we can think of the Spirit of God as creatively present to every creature, dwelling in each, surrounding it with love, holding it in a community of creation and accompanying it in its life and in its death. In the Spirit, God dwells in, knows, and loves each individual creature. As the Wisdom of Solomon tells us, God creates out of love. Creatures exist because God loves them. They are called forth and held in existence only out of love (Wis 11:24-26). In our own best moments we human beings can find ourselves capable of feeling with individual nonhuman creatures. This can give us a glimpse into the Creator's feeling for things. We are surely right to think that our human experience of compassion for nonhuman creatures is but the palest reflection of the divine compassion. The God of radical compassion revealed in Jesus can be understood as a God who knows each creature's experience, delights in each, suffers with each, and embraces each in love. This is a God who cares about individuals, not just the big picture. God is a God not just of the ecological whole but also of the individual organism.

2. Each sparrow is inscribed in the eternal life of God by the Holy Spirit. Paul tells us that it is the Spirit of God who brings resurrection life to human beings: "If the Spirit who raised Jesus from the dead dwells in you, he who raised Jesus from the dead will give life to your mortal bodies also through his Spirit that dwells in you" (Rom 8:11). He also thinks of this same Spirit as at work in creation as it groans in labor pains and waits "with eager longing" for its fulfillment (Rom 8:19-23). Because the Holy Spirit is the immanent one, the one who comes close to each creature in love, and the one who mediates the power of resurrection life, I think it can be said that it is through the Spirit that creatures are inscribed in the divine life. Jesus tells his disciples to rejoice that their names are written in heaven (Luke 10:20). The idea of a "Book of Life" is widespread in the biblical tradition (Exod 32:32; Ps 56:8; 69:28; 139:16; Job 19:23; Mal 3:16-18; Phil 4:3; Rev 20:12-14; 21:27). Based on God's fidelity to what God creates, and on the eternal nature of the love that God has for each creature, there is every reason to think that the image of the Book of Life can be applied in a differentiated way to all God's creatures. As human beings are inscribed in their personal way in the Book of Life, so, in their own distinctive ways, other creatures are eternally inscribed in the life of God through the life-giving Spirit.[29] The Spirit is not to be thought of as abandoning the sparrow that falls to the ground, but as gathering it up, inscribing it eternally in the life of the Trinity, bringing it into the realm of redemptive life in Christ.

3. Each sparrow participates in redemption in Christ. I am taking "redemption" as pointing not only to forgiveness of sin, which is a matter of great importance to human beings, but also to the final liberation and fulfillment of nonhuman creatures. It is taken in the wide sense of the recapitulation (Eph 1:10) of all things in Christ and the reconciliation (Col 1:20) of the whole of creation in Christ. The Christian tradition has seen the risen Christ as the one in whom the wounded will find healing and the poor and oppressed be raised up and it expressed this conviction in the concept of the last judgment. The idea of the last judgment has understandably fallen from favor because it has been used to instill terror, but I believe it needs to be rediscovered as the assurance that evil will be both acknowledged and rejected and that good will not be lost but be taken up into God. In the last judgment, the crucified one can be thought of as bringing healing, by revealing and responding to the wounds of the victim and the shame of the perpetrator.[30] In particular, I am proposing that the last judgment needs to be rediscovered as expressing hope for the healing of the whole of creation in Christ. It is the risen Christ who says "Behold I make all things new" (Rev 21:5). But the question remains: How is this transformation of creation to be further understood?

4. *Each sparrow can be thought of as eternally held in the living memory of the Trinity.* The dynamic, shared life of God can be thought of as involving the holding and treasuring of every creature of every time in the living present of the Trinity. The Christian tradition gives a central place to sacred memory (*anamnesis*). When Christians gather for the Eucharist, they remember what God has done in the life, death, and resurrection of Jesus. This kind of eucharistic remembering is far from being simply a memory of the past. It functions powerfully and realistically in the present. It both promises and anticipates the divine communion. It brings those gathered into living communion with Jesus Christ and makes them participants in divine trinitarian communion. This experience may provide a pale analogy for God's redemptive and living memory of a sparrow or a dinosaur. What is being suggested here is that God is not only with each individual creature in its lifetime, inscribing it eternally in the Spirit and bringing it to redemptive fulfillment in Christ, but also celebrating it in the living memory and experience

of the trinitarian life. In the communion of saints, human beings can be thought of as coming to share the divine delight in and treasuring of the existence and contribution of an individual dinosaur. The communion of saints would then be thought of as opening up to the communion of all creation. The capacity we already have to treasure all that makes up the history of life offers a hint of the treasuring that is possible in the life of the divine communion. In this proposal, individual creatures are taken up into the living experience of trinitarian God. They abide permanently within the everlasting compassionate love of the Three. They are celebrated, respected, and honored in the communion of saints. John Haught speaks of the whole of creation as being redeemed by being taken up into the enduring divine experience of the world. He says that everything in creation, "all the suffering and tragedy as well as the emergence of new life and intense beauty," is being *saved* by "being taken eternally into God's feeling for the world."[31] Individual creatures can be understood as taken up in the living experience of God. They abide permanently within the everlasting compassion of God.

5. *Is the individual sparrow that falls to the ground fulfilled in a way that is appropriate to its nature by being taken up into the living memory of the Trinity? Or is it finally fulfilled by some further form of participation in resurrection life?* I have argued above that every individual animal and bird will be taken up into God, and I have suggested that we can think of this occurring as each creature is loved and held in the living memory of the Trinity. There is good reason to think that the redemption of individual creatures occurs *at least* in this way. I take this to be a minimalist view of the future of individual sparrows. But is there more? It can certainly be affirmed that the wisdom of God will respect the particular nature that is specific to the creature. This suggests that what is appropriate fulfillment for a human being may not be appropriate to a crab, a mosquito, or a bacterium. Jürgen Moltmann has envisaged God's eschatological action as involving a literal waking and a gathering of every creature of every time. He sees Christ as coming in glory to raise up creatures

of all times simultaneously, in a single instant.[32] This proposal is a brave one, but it is highly speculative and hard to imagine. I am more inclined to be reserved about the mental picture of redeemed creation. It seems to me that we do not know whether, in the divine wisdom, some kind of resurrection is the *appropriate* fulfillment of an individual dinosaur. Elizabeth Johnson has rightly insisted on how little we know about what lies beyond death. Our ultimate hope is based not on information about the future but on "the character of God" revealed in the Christ-event.[33] What we know about this divine character is that it is radically faithful and eternally loving. What we do not know, I believe, is whether an individual sparrow will find its appropriate fulfillment in the living memory of the Trinity, which is surely far more powerful, healing, and liberating than anything we can imagine, or whether God will find it appropriate to raise up the sparrow in some other way.

What can be said with confidence, based on the character of God revealed in the Christ-event, is that individual animals and birds will be taken up into the eternal divine life. The God of resurrection life is a God who brings individual creatures in their own distinctiveness *in some way* into the eternal dynamic life of the divine communion.

I have been proposing that each creature, each little sparrow, is known and loved by God, is eternally inscribed in God by the Holy Spirit, participates in redemption in Christ, and is eternally held and treasured in the life of the Trinity. The diverse range of creatures that springs from the abundance of this divine communion finds redemption in being taken up eternally into this communion. Because God relates to each creature on its own terms, final fulfillment will fit the nature of each creature. There is every reason to believe that individual creatures will find their proper redemption in the divine communion in a way that we cannot fully articulate.

7

Worship and Practice

How do ecological issues such as global climate change impact on our celebrations of the Eucharist? How is eucharistic worship related to ecological action and life-styles? What is it to live an ecological vocation before the God of Jesus Christ? What is the relationship between ecological practice and Christian spirituality? In this last chapter I attempt a response to these questions, taking up, first, some suggestions for an ecological theology of the Eucharist, and then some reflections on spirituality and praxis.

Toward an Ecological Theology of the Eucharist

The proposal advanced in this section is that, when Christians gather for the Eucharist, they bring the Earth and all its creatures, and in some way the whole universe, to the table. I will explore this proposal by working through fives steps: Eucharist (1) as the lifting up of all creation, (2) as the living memory of both creation and redemption, (3) as sacrament of the cosmic Christ, (4) as participation with all God's creatures in the communion of the Trinity, and (5) as solidarity with the victims of climate change and other ecological crises.

The Lifting Up of All Creation

John Zizioulas, a distinguished theologian and bishop of the Ecumenical Patriarchate of the Orthodox Church, has spelled out his ecological theology in a series of lectures given at Kings College

London.[1] He argues that the ecological crisis cannot be met simply by arguments based on reason. While these clearly have their place, far more is required. Zizioulas insists that, if we hope to change priorities and life-styles, we will need a different *culture* and a different *ethos*. As a Christian theologian, Zizioulas is convinced that what is needed above all is a *liturgical* ethos. While ecological conversion can be inspired by many sources besides Christianity, I think Zizioulas is right in seeing the Christian community as possessing a unique foundation for a radically ecological ethos in its eucharistic spirituality.

Like many Orthodox theologians, he sees human beings as called by God to be "priests of creation." He distinguishes this priestly task from notions of sacrificial priesthood that he associates with medieval and Roman Catholic theology. He sees each baptized person as called to be, like Christ, a fully *personal* being. This involves being relational rather than self-enclosed, being able to go out of self to the other, in what he calls *ek-stasis*. Persons are always ecstatic, in the sense that they achieve personhood only in communion with others. Humans are relational beings. Their vocation is to relate in a fully personal way to God, to other humans, and to other creatures of God. According to Zizioulas, humanity and the rest of creation come to their completion in the life of God through each other.

When humans come to the Eucharist, they bring the fruits of creation, and in some way the whole creation, to the eucharistic table. In the Eucharist, creation is *lifted up* to God in offering and thanksgiving. In the East, the central eucharistic prayer is known as the Anaphora, a word that means the lifting-up. The gifts of creation are lifted up to God, and the Spirit is invoked to transform the gifts of creation and the assembled community into the body of Christ. The exercise of this priesthood is not confined to the ordained but is the God-given role of all the faithful. It is not restricted to liturgical celebrations but is meant to happen in the whole of life. It involves all human interactions with the rest of creation. The "lifting up" of creation is meant to be played out around the planet continually by every human being. Fundamentally this priestly task is nothing other than an authentic personal love for other creatures in all their specificity, a fully human feeling for them and celebration of them in God. Our stance toward the rest of creation, our personal engagement with it as fully relational beings, is a central dimension of our life before God and salvation in Christ.

The ecological crisis requires the deepest resources of the human community. With Zizioulas, I believe that in the Eucharist Christians have a profound source for an authentically ecological ethos and culture.[2] Christian eucharistic practice, when understood and lived in all its depth, is capable of sustaining an ongoing conversion to a personal and loving stance before the rest of creation. It does not provide answers to the practical questions that confront us, but it does offer a motivation and a genuinely ecological ethos.[3]

The Living Memory of Both Creation and Redemption

The concept of *anamnesis* is central to eucharistic theology. This Greek word can be translated as "a memorial" or simply as "memory," but I think it is best translated as "living memory." In every Eucharist, we remember the events of our salvation in Christ, in such a way that they are made present to us powerfully here and now and anticipate the future transformation of all things in Christ. This kind of memory not only recalls the past but acts powerfully in the present and opens out toward God's future. In the Eucharist, the Christian community naturally focuses on Christ's liberating death and resurrection, but what is often forgotten is that every Eucharist is a thanksgiving memorial for God at work in creation as well as in redemption.

Long ago Louis Bouyer pointed out that the early Christian eucharistic prayers had their origins and models in Jewish prayer forms used in synagogues and especially in homes, above all in the Passover meal.[4] These prayers begin with a blessing of the gifts of creation. They are based on the memory of and thanksgiving for God's work, which involves both creation and salvation. Both Jewish prayer forms and the early Christian eucharistic prayers involve an *anamnesis* of creation and redemption.[5] Zizioulas makes the same point, insisting that all the ancient eucharistic liturgies began with thanksgiving for *creation* and then continued with thanksgiving for *redemption* in Christ, and all of them were centered on the lifting up of the gifts of creation to the Creator.[6]

This is of fundamental importance in a time when human action is radically altering the climate with disastrous effects for human beings and for other creatures on Earth. When we come to the Eucharist we bring the creatures of Earth with us. We remember the God who loves each one of them. We grieve for the damage done to them. We feel with them. We can begin to learn the kind of ethos that Zizioulas speaks of, an ethos that leads to a different way of acting.

This ancient theology is still found in current liturgical texts. In every Eucharist, we begin by bringing creation to the table, bread and wine, "fruit of the Earth and the work of human hands."[7] Our everyday eucharistic prayers bring out the inner relationship between God's action in creation and redemption: "He is the Word through whom you made the universe, the Saviour you sent to redeem us" (Second Eucharistic Prayer). They make it clear that when we come to the Eucharist we bring creation with us and praise God on behalf of all of Earth's creatures: "All creation rightly gives you praise" (Third Eucharistic Prayer); "In the name of every creature under heaven, we too praise your glory" (Fourth Eucharistic Prayer).

In every Eucharist, we remember the events of Christ's life, death, and resurrection and experience their power to bring healing and salvation. We also remember God's good creation, the fourteen-billion-year history of the universe, the 4.7-billion-year history of Earth and the emergence of life on Earth in all its diversity and beauty. We remember the vulnerable state of the community of life on Earth today and bring this to God. All of this is caught up in the mystery of Christ celebrated in each of our Eucharists. In the great doxology at the end of the eucharistic prayer, we lift up the whole creation through, with, and in Christ, "in the unity of the Holy Spirit" to the eternal praise and glory of God.[8]

Sacrament of the Cosmic Christ

The Christ we encounter in the Eucharist is the risen one, the one in whom all things were created and in whom all are reconciled (Col 1:15-20). God's eternal wisdom and plan for the fullness of time is "to gather up all things in him, things in heaven and things on earth" (Eph 1:10). Even when, in the Eucharist, the focus of the memorial is on Christ's death and resurrection, this is not a memory that takes us away from creation. On the contrary, it involves us directly with creation. It connects us to Earth and all its creatures.

When we remember Christ's death, we remember a creature of our universe, part of the interconnected evolutionary history of our planet, freely handing his whole bodily and personal existence into the mystery of a loving God. When we remember the resurrection, we remember part of our universe and part of our evolutionary history being taken up in the Spirit into God. This is the beginning of the transformation of the whole creation in Christ. As Rahner says, this resurrection of Jesus is not only the *promise* but the *beginning* of the glorification and divinization of the whole of reality.[9]

The Eucharist is the symbol and the sacrament of the risen Christ who is the beginning of the transfiguration of all creatures in God. In eating and drinking at this table we participate in the risen Christ (1 Cor 10:16-17). Bread and wine are the sacrament of the Christ who is at work in creation. According to Christian faith, what is symbolized is wonderfully made present. And what is made present is Christ in the power of resurrection, as not only the promise but also the beginning of the transformation of all things. Every Eucharist is both sign and agent of the transforming work of the risen Christ in the whole of creation.

I believe that this kind of sacramental theology is the context for interpreting for today the prayer of Teilhard de Chardin in his *Mass on the World*:

All the things in the world to which this day will bring increase; all those that will diminish; all those too that will die: all of them, Lord, I try to gather into my arms, so as to hold them out to you in offering. This is the material of my sacrifice; the only material you desire. . . . Over every living thing which is to spring up, to grow, to flower, to ripen during this day say again the words: This is my Body. And over every death-force which waits in readiness to corrode, to wither, to cut down, speak again your commanding words which express the supreme mystery of faith: This is my Blood.[10]

As Teilhard's prayer unfolds, he sees the power of God at work in Christ and present in the Eucharist as transforming the Earth from within. Because the Word is made flesh, no part of the physical universe is untouched. All matter is the place of God. All is being divinized. All is being transformed in Christ: "Through your own incarnation, my God, all matter is henceforth incarnate."[11] Because of this, Earth, the solar system, and the whole universe become the place for encounter with the risen Christ: "Now, Lord, through the consecration of the world the luminosity and fragrance which suffuse the universe take on for me the lineaments of a body and a face—in you."

The Eucharist is an effective prayer for the transformation of the universe in Christ. It points toward and anticipates the divinization of the universe in Christ. The one we encounter sacramentally in the Eucharist is the one in whom all things were created and in whom all will be transfigured. Human action, which is an expression of love and respect for the living creatures, the atmosphere, the seas, and the land of our planet, can be seen as not only in continuity with, but also in some way part of, the work of the eucharistic Christ. Willfully contributing to the destruction of species, or to pumping more and more carbon dioxide into the atmosphere, must be seen as a denial of Christ. It is a denial of the meaning of all that we celebrate when we gather for the Eucharist.

Participating with All God's Creatures in Trinitarian Communion

Every Eucharist is an eschatological event, an event of the Spirit that anticipates the future when all things will be taken up into divine communion. The Eucharist is profoundly trinitarian. Our eucharistic communion, our communion with each other in Christ, is always a sharing in and a tasting of the divine communion of the Trinity, in which all things will be transfigured and find their eternal meaning and their true home. This trinitarian communion which we share is the source of all life on Earth; it is what enables a community of life to emerge and evolve; and, in ways that are beyond our imagination and comprehension, it is what will be the fulfillment of all the creatures of our planet, and all the wonders of our universe. As we participate in the Eucharist, we taste in anticipation the fulfillment of all things taken up into the divine life of the Trinity.

This means, as Tony Kelly has said, that the "most intense moment of our communion with God is at the same time an intense moment of our communion with the earth."[12] By being taken up into God, we are caught up into God's love for the creatures of our planetary community. This begins to shape our ecological imagination: "The Eucharist educates the imagination, the mind, and the heart to apprehend the universe as one of communion and connectedness in Christ." In this eucharistic imagination, a distinctive ecological vision and commitment can take shape.[13] With this kind of imagination at work in us, we can see the other creatures of Earth as our kin, as radically interconnected with us in one Earth community of life before God. We can begin to see critically—to see more clearly what is happening to the Earth. We are led to participate in God's feeling for the life-forms of our planet. An authentic eucharistic imagination leads to an ecological ethos, culture, and praxis.

Solidarity with Victims

The Eucharist always involves the memory of the cross. The theologian Johann Baptist Metz speaks of this as a "dangerous" memory.[14] The cross of Jesus is an abiding challenge to all complacency before the suffering of others. It brings those who suffer to the very center of Christian faith. It challenges self-serving and ideological justifications of the misery of the poor and the victims of war, oppression, and natural disasters. The resurrection offers a dynamic vision of hope for the suffering of the world, but it does not dull the memory of the suffering ones. They are always present, forever imaged in the wounds of the risen Christ.

This dangerous and critical memory provides an alternative way of seeing and acting. It leads to solidarity, to alternative life-styles, and to personal and political action. The World Council of Churches, in its reflections on solidarity with victims of climate change, points to the many communities of people, especially in the Southern Hemisphere, who are particularly vulnerable to climate change: "Though their per capita contribution to the causes of climate change is negligible, they will suffer from the consequences to a much larger degree."[15] Climate change and other aspects of our ecological crisis aggravate the social and economic inequity between rich and poor in our global community. To contribute to this destruction of lives, of homes, of livelihoods, and of communities "is not only a sin against the weak and unprotected but also against the earth—God's gift of life."[16]

The Eucharist, as a living memory of all those who suffer, calls the Christian community to a new solidarity that involves all the human victims as well as the animals and plants that are destroyed or threatened. Solidarity involves personal and political commitment to both of the two strategies that have been identified as responses to climate change—*mitigation* and *adaptation*. Adaptation will mean reordering society, budgeting in readiness for ecological disasters, training personnel, and allocating resources. In a particular way it will involve, as a matter of justice, hospitality to environmental refugees.

When we Australian Christians gather for eucharistic celebrations, we gather in solidarity with Christians who assemble for Eucharist in Kiribas, in Tuvalu, and in Bangladesh. We gather in solidarity with those who share other forms of religious faith in the Pacific, in Southeast Asia, in Africa, and in all parts of our global community. We remember those already displaced from their homes and their heritage. We cannot but be painfully aware of the threat to many millions of other people. We are challenged to be mindful of Australia's contribution to greenhouse gases, of our wealth created by coal, of our use of motor vehicles. We pray in solidarity with the global community that the Eucharist that brings us into peace and communion with God may "advance the peace and salvation of all the world" (Third Eucharistic Prayer). We commit ourselves again to discipleship, to an ecological ethos, lifestyle, politics, and praxis, as people of Easter hope.

Peter Scott has said that in the Eucharist, "the eucharistic community is bound in sociality to the wider ecological society, and interprets and clarifies it." He describes the Eucharist as an event of divine hospitality and points out that this hospitality "has no ecclesiastical restrictions, and encompasses the non-human."[17] He sees the Eucharist as a powerful political resource that Christianity offers to an ecological age. In every Eucharist, we gather in one place with all our ordinariness and limitations. We take up the fruits of the earth and the work of human hands. We encounter Jesus, in all the healing, liberating love poured out in his life and death and know again his presence as the risen one transforming all things from within. In the power of the Spirit, we participate in and taste the eschatological communion of the Trinity. In the Spirit, the assembly is made one in Christ, in a communion in God that has no borders but reaches out to embrace all of God's creatures. Every Eucharist calls us to ecological conversion and action.

Spirituality and Practice

Conversion is central to Christian life. It is never something that is done. It always appears before us again as an invitation and a grace offered in the new circumstances that we face. As Brennan Hill says, "Christian spirituality is a journey on the earth that constantly calls for conversion and maturing."[18] This book has been an extended argument that the following of Jesus in the twenty-first century will involve ongoing ecological conversion. The scope and intensity of the ecological crisis challenge us in a radical way. No other generation has had to face up to human-induced global climate change, and the knowledge that their action or inaction will determine the future of life on the planet. As Sean McDonagh points out, no other generation has had to accept responsibility for the survival of the biodiversity of the planet:

> The task quite simply is to take decisive action to stave off the extinction of species which could sterilize the planet. If this generation does not act, no future generation will be able to undo the damage that this generation has caused to the planet. It is an extraordinary and awesome moment that the behaviour of a single generation of humans can have such a profound and irreversible impact, not just on human history, but on the life of the planet as well.[19]

The ecological conversion to which we are called involves a new way of seeing, thinking, and acting. Whether one's meaning system be that of Judaism, Islam, Buddhism, Christianity, Indigenous Australian religious traditions, or some form of humanism, the state of the planet is a challenge to a profound conversion that involves mind and heart, life-style and politics. I suspect that each of the great religious traditions has within itself resources for this work of ongoing conversion, and I believe that it demands a response from all of our traditions and collaboration among all of them. My hope is that this book might function as a partial sketch of how this work of ecological conversion can find inspiration from within the tradition of Christian faith, as part of this wider conversation.

The Way of Wisdom

Those who understand their lives as a following of Jesus see him not only as the one who lived in Galilee two thousand years ago, proclaiming the compassion of God and the coming reign of God in words and deeds, but also as the Wisdom of God, the eternal Word made flesh, the crucified and risen one who is the beginning of the transformation of the whole creation. I am proposing that discipleship of Jesus means following the way of wisdom and that this involves loving respect for all of God's creatures. I will not attempt an ecological ethics from the perspective of Wisdom, something taken up by Celia Deane-Drummond in a number of works,[20] but simply sketch a theological approach to ecological praxis.

Paul not only sees Jesus crucified as the true wisdom of God (1 Cor 1:24, 30) but also sees human beings as participating in true wisdom, because in Christ they find the revelation of God's hidden purpose in creation (1 Cor 2:7-10). We humans can possess wisdom, but it comes as a gift, the gift of the Spirit who "searches everything, even the depths of God" (1 Cor 2:10). In Ephesians we read: "with all wisdom and insight God has made known to us the mystery of his will, according to his good pleasure that he set forth in Christ, to gather up all things in himself, things in heaven and on earth" (Eph 1:8-10). Wisdom is "the plan of the mystery hidden for all ages in God who created all things" (Eph 3:9-10). We participate in this divine wisdom by an enlightening of the "eyes of the heart" that allows us to know the hope to which we are called (Eph 1:18). The basis of this hope is the risen Christ at work in the universe beyond all cosmic powers (Eph 1:22-23).[21]

The way of wisdom involves both enlightenment and action. It is an enlightenment that bears fruit in action. Enlightenment springs from the hope we possess that all will be taken up and transfigured in the risen Christ. It is a seeing and valuing of all things in relation to Christ and faithful action in the light of this. To follow Jesus-Wisdom is to see every sparrow as held and loved by God. It is also to see every sparrow and every great soaring tree as created in the Wisdom of God that is made flesh in Jesus of Nazareth. To live in wisdom, in the full Christian sense, means seeing the whole of creation as coming forth from the dynamic abundance of the Trinity, as evolving within the dynamism of the life of the Three, and as destined to find fulfillment in this shared life.

Bonaventure tells us that every creature is "nothing less than a kind of representation of the wisdom of God." He sees each creature as a work of art produced by the divine artist and as reflecting this artist: "Every creature is of its nature a likeness and resemblance to eternal wisdom."[22] The human practice of true wisdom, then, involves seeing each creature in its relationship to its eternal origin and destiny. This way of seeing specific creatures in God is what Bonaventure calls "contuition." It is important to note that this is not a bypassing of the specificity and particularity of the individual creature but an embracing of each in its uniqueness and in its unique relationship to the living God.

The way of wisdom can be understood as the way of loving knowledge, of "knowledge through love."[23] It is the fruit of the Spirit of love at work in us. To act wisely is not only to act in accord with all the available empirical evidence, but also to act in a way that is at one with the gift of the Spirit breathing through creation and breathing love in us. Loving knowledge is the kind of knowing we have of a beloved friend. It is not a love that claims to comprehend or to control the other, but a love that recognizes the other, even in the intimacy of deep friendship, as an abiding mystery. This kind of loving knowledge is the essential foundation for ecological practice. It is a stance before reality that challenges the absolute claims made by the economics of the free market, on the one hand, and by certain forms of science and technology, on the other. There are, of course, times when we need to struggle to comprehend what confronts us, whether it be in mathematics, biology, economics, politics, or theology. But the knowledge that seeks and claims comprehension and control can be a dangerous knowledge. It needs to be situated in a fundamental stance before reality that recognizes the limits of what we can claim to know, that accepts the mystery of the other in humility.

There is a wisdom saying of Jesus that speaks of the importance of a sound eye: "The eye is the lamp of the body. So if the eye is healthy, your whole body will be full of light; but if your eye is unhealthy, your whole body will be full of darkness" (Matt 6:22). A sound eye, seeing things rightly, is of the essence of the way of wisdom. Sallie McFague contrasts the "arrogant eye" with the "loving eye." The arrogant eye is characteristic of the typical Western attitude to the natural world. It objectifies, manipulates, uses, and exploits. The loving eye does not come automatically to us. It requires training and discipline to see things with a loving eye. McFague points out that the loving eye requires detachment in order to see the difference, distinctiveness, and uniqueness of the other. Too often we imagine that we know who or what the other is, instead of taking the trouble to find out. McFague writes:

This is the eye trained in detachment in order that its attachment will be objective, based on the reality of the other and not on its own wishes or fantasies. This is the eye bound to the other as is an apprentice to a skilled worker, listening to the other as does a foreigner in a new country. This is the eye that pays attention to the other so that the connections between knower and known, like the bond of friendship, will be on the real subject in its real world.[24]

What is required is that we learn to love others, human and non-human, with a love that involves both distance and intimacy. This involves cultivating a loving eye that respects difference. This is the way of wisdom, a way of seeing each creature in relation to God, as a unique manifestation of divine Wisdom, as embraced by God in the incarnation and destined to share in the redemption of all things in Christ.

Praxis in the Spirit

The way of wisdom involves praxis—the combination of active engagement and ongoing reflection that is at the heart of all liberation theology. Conversion to the Earth, to solidarity with the creatures that make up our planetary community, must involve action. It is not only a radical reorientation of thought, and it is not only the discovery of a new capacity for feeling for nonhuman creation. It is both of these issuing forth in personal, political, and ecclesial action.

To follow Jesus means being led by the Spirit as he was Spirit-led at every stage of his journey. This involves a truly personal discernment, but it is never an individualistic one. The Spirit of God is always the Spirit of communion, communion with our human sisters and brothers and communion with the whole of creation. It is not difficult to see the Spirit at work in great movements of our times—the ecological movement, the movement seeking justice and peace above all for the poor of the Earth, and the feminist movement seeking the full equality of women. In spite of all the human failures and sin that play a role in these movements, they are places where the Spirit of God is powerfully at work, calling us to our own part in these movements of liberation and hope.

To be led by the Spirit at the beginning of the twenty-first century is to be involved with what Thomas Berry describes the "Great Work." This Great Work is to carry out the transition from "a period of human devastation of the Earth" to a period when humans will "be present to the planet in a mutually beneficial manner."[25] To make this transition will mean expanding our moral community. David Toolan says that "we need to expand our moral concern to include plants, animals, air and water and soils." We need to recognize that we are one species among others, but, at the same time, we must accept responsibility for the future of the planet: "leaving nature alone is simply not a viable option."[26] Morality must now mean accepting responsibility for climate change, for the state of the fisheries, and for the future of the Earth's rain forests.

Toolan locates this ethical challenge in the deeper place of the human being's role in the emerging universe and in the evolutionary history of life on Earth. It is as if the stardust in our DNA, the microbes that swim in our cells, the bacteria that gave us a breathable atmosphere all now wait upon human beings to finish the great cosmic symphony. It is only with us, with *Homo sapiens*, that the atoms born in stars can become mindful of the meaning of things, so that they can begin to decipher "the mystery hidden from the foundation of the world."[27] Toolan says that human beings are called to give soul to the universe:

> We are great mothering nature's soul-space, her heart and vocal chords—and her willingness, if we consent to it, to be spirited, to be the vessel of the Holy One whose concern reaches out to embrace all that is created. When we fail in this soul-work, fail in extending our own reach of concern, nature fails/falls with us. But when it happens, when we say yes to the Spirit who hovers over our inner chaos, the mountains clap their hands, the hills leap like gazelles. They and the quarks have a big stake in us.[28]

Human creatures are the ones who can consciously give praise, who can lift up creation to God in love. As Sean McDonagh, one of the prophets of ecological praxis, says, "our unique human vocation is to celebrate the beauty and fruitfulness of all life on Earth."[29] Christian ecological action is grounded in celebration. It is grounded in the Eucharist. But it issues forth in personal and political action. Paul Santmire reclaims the tradition of the martyrs for ecological theology, pointing out that to be a martyr means to be a witness. He sees the church of today, empowered and driven by the Spirit, as challenged to rise to the occasion of these times—as martyrs in other eras rose to the occasions that were thrust upon them. The challenge is to allow the love of God in Christ Jesus "so to pour into our hearts by the indwelling of the Holy Spirit that it overflows abundantly, not only to persons, especially to those in great need, but also to the other creatures of nature." We need a new form of the martyr church:

> How then will this martyr church in the ecological and cosmic age love nature? Passionately and persistently and pervasively. We Christians will be a voice for the voiceless, for the sake of all creatures of nature who have no voice in human affairs. We will listen to the plaintive cries of the great whales and hear the groaning of the rain forests, and we will be their advocates in the village squares and in the courts of power, by the grace of God. All the more will we hear the bitter wailing of the little children who live on the trash mountains of this world and who wear clothes that have been washed in streams overflowing with heinous poisons and who sometimes drink these very waters.[30]

The witness of the Christian community will be carried out in workplaces, in neighborhoods, and in homes, and sometimes in political and activist groups. It can and must be lived in the very way we go about our daily lives, in every trade and profession and in every home. Very often the praxis of individual Christians will be done in collaboration with others far removed from the life of the church. But, as I think Santmire is suggesting, there is also a place for ecclesial action where the church itself witnesses in the public arena through its structures of leadership.

Two recent simple examples of this come to mind. On World Ocean Day, June 8, 2004, the seven Catholic Bishops of the state of Queensland in Australia issued a pastoral letter on the threatened and damaged Great Barrier Reef. They celebrated the reef, with its coral trout, huge groupers, sea snakes, large green turtles, humpback whales, sea grasses, sea fern, sponges, and anemones as a beautiful gift of God that arouses wonder, gratitude, and praise. They assessed the serious dangers facing the reef and called their people to take responsibility for its survival and its health.[31] Then, on the feast of St. Francis of Assisi, October 4, 2004, eleven bishops of the Murray-Darling Basin endorsed a statement of Catholic Earthcare Australia that supports political action on salinity and increased river flow and calls for commitment to conserving and reusing water.[32] What is important about these examples (and a number of others from around the world) is that (1) the response is local, involving local church leaders taking a position on ecological issues that arise in their own bioregion, and (2) in adopting political options, such as increased environmental river flow, the bishops are not only defending the good of human beings but also explicitly extending their moral commitment and advocacy to include the animals, plants, and fish of the Murray-Darling and the Great Barrier Reef.

Listening to the Spirit may well lead Christian believers to get involved in political action through activist and lobbying groups. In my view, it will certainly involve a critical challenge to the dominant economic and political model based on market forces and endless consumption. It will mean accepting that the resources of the Earth are finite, that current Western consumption patterns cannot be sustained by the wider human community, or into future generations, and that they bring death and destruction to other species in our planetary community of life. It will mean personal and political options in support of renewable sources of energy, alternative forms of transport, the conservation and reuse of water, the designing of energy-efficient buildings, the protection of habitats, the limitation of urban sprawl, and the attempt to bring life and beauty to our cities. It many instances, it will mean living more consciously and more fully in a local area, in a particular bioregion, and in a local human community with its local businesses and its local life.

A Mysticism of Ecological Praxis

To be converted to a sense of kinship with and responsibility for the creatures of Earth, and for the land, atmosphere, seas, and rivers that support them, can be a joyful and liberating experience. Getting involved with the struggle for a more just and ecologically sustainable world can be fulfilling and meaningful, an experience of communion with other human beings and with the natural world. It may involve the experience of success, a habitat saved, a conservation park established, an international protocol on carbon emissions accepted, but it will certainly also involve suffering and the experience of failure. This can lead to a sense of hopelessness, because of the sheer power of the economic and political forces that are committed to maximum short-term profits with no regard for ecological or social consequences.

Christian hope is based on God, on God's self-bestowal in Christ, and the promise that all is taken up in Christ and will be transfigured in him. Our own commitments, our own actions, our successes, and our failures will become the raw material for this final transformation. Saving species, saving habitats matters before God. Our struggles have final and eternal meaning. Individual creatures have final meaning before God.

This meaning, this promise matters greatly in the midst of our commitments and actions. But more is needed if hope is to be kept alive. We need to be anchored in the promise of God as a matter of experience. We need to be mystics. Karl Rahner has said a number of times that the Christian of the future will be a mystic or he or she will cease to be anything at all.[33] Of course, what Rahner has in mind is not mysticism understood as some form of visionary or trance-like experience. Nor is he thinking primarily of the experience of quiet, contemplative prayer before God—although this is certainly part of the picture. What he has in mind is what he calls the "the mysticism of everyday life."[34] He believes that, by God's grace, there is an experience of God that occurs in every life, and at the heart of life, whether this be noticed and named or not. It may occur in the deep unquenchable longing of the heart, in the quest for answers that opens up more and more questions, in the experience of truly radical commitment to a cause, in the utter pain of loss and grief where something enables us to endure and go on, in small acts of love that spring from a radical commitment of oneself. In such experiences there is an openness to mystery, to the transcendent, that Christians call the experience of grace. In the light of Christian revelation we can see this as the place of the Holy Spirit in our lives, we can open our beings to the one who is silently present at the center of our experience. This is the mysticism of daily life.

What I think we need for the twenty-first century is what might be called a mysticism of ecological praxis. The liberation theologians of the twentieth century and their European counterparts came to recognize that Christians committed to the cause of political liberation need to be both political and mystical. It is only the mystical that can enable us to hope against hope, to act with integrity, and to love in the political and the personal spheres in times of adversity and failure, up to and including death. Edward Schillebeeckx sums up this when he says that authentic faith, or the mystical, seems in modern times "to be nurtured above all in and through the praxis of liberation." In this experience there grows the awareness that God is revealed as "the deepest mystery, the heart and the soul of any truly human liberation."[35] He points out that the political form of love of God and neighbor knows the same need for repentance and conversion, the same asceticism, the same sufferings and dark nights, as is the case in contemplative mysticism.[36] He says: "Without prayer or mysticism politics soon becomes cruel and barbaric. Without political love, prayer or mysticism soon becomes sentimental or uncommitted interiority."[37]

The challenge to find the living God in solidarity with the poor of the Earth remains an enormous challenge for Christian faith in this coming century. The argument of this book is that commitment to the poor and commitment to the well-being of life on this planet must go together as two interrelated dimensions of the one Christian vocation. Ecological conversion is not opposed to, but intimately involved with, conversion to the side of the poor. And ecological conversion, like conversion to the side of the poor, will need to involve both the political and the mystical, and the discovery of the mystical precisely in the political.

What then would a mysticism of ecological praxis look like? I suggest that it might embrace some of these kinds of experiences:

- The experience of being caught up in the utter beauty of the natural world, when this leads to a wonder and a joy that seem boundless.
- The experience of being part of a fourteen-billion-year history of the universe, and part of a 3.8-billion-year history of the evolution of life on Earth, and of knowing all this as directed to God's self-bestowal in love.
- The experience of being overwhelmed by natural forces, by the size and age of the universe, of knowing the natural world as other, of feeling it as alien, and in this being taken far beyond human comfort zones into mystery.
- The experience of being called to solidarity with the creatures of Earth, of being called to an ecological conversion, of coming to know other creatures as kin, and of knowing this as the gracious gift of the Spirit of God.
- The experience of being overwhelmed by the size of the ecological problem, of being defeated by powerful economic forces, of seeing rain forests further destroyed, more species go extinct, more carbon pumped into the atmosphere, of feeling near despair, but still hoping against hope, of knowing this as a participation in the way of this cross, as an invitation to commit ourselves to go on, entrusting ourselves and our damaged Earth into the hands of God.
- The experience of conversion from the model of individualism and consumption to the simplicity of what Sallie McFague calls "life abundant" and knowing in this the truth of God: where what matters are the basic necessities of food, clothes, shelter, medical care, educational opportunities, loving relationships, meaningful work, an enriching imaginative and spiritual life, time with friends, and time spent with the natural world around us.[38]
- The experience of commitment to the creatures of our Earth community that takes us beyond our tendencies to self-righteousness and self-satisfaction, that has the character of a life-long, in fact, an eternal commitment, which we can recognize as sheer grace.

8

Ecology at the Heart
of Christian Faith

This has been a journey through some central aspects of Christian faith. In each chapter I have attempted to show how an important part of the Christian tradition can be rethought as a contemporary ecological theology. My hope is that this kind of theology can make a contribution to the ecological conversion to which Christians, along with the rest of humanity, are called. By way of conclusion, I will bring together some of the key ideas of the book in a series of summary statements.

Human Beings within the Community of Creation: "Made in the Image of God"

- Humans, with all the other living creatures of Earth, are formed from the hydrogen of the Big Bang, and from elements such as carbon that are forged in the nuclear furnaces of stars and evolve from the first bacterial forms of life that emerged on our planet 3.8 billion years ago.
- Within the community of creation, human beings are made in the image of God in the sense that they are part of creation that has come to personhood, they are invited into interpersonal relationship with God in grace, and they are called to graceful relations with their fellow creatures.
- Humans are called to see themselves as "kin" with other creatures in a community of God's creation. They are also called to use their human creativity, intelligence, and wisdom to "cultivate and take

119

care of" God's creation (Gen 2:15). The conversion implied in the kinship model is the crucial prerequisite for cultivating and caring for creation.

The Creator Spirit: "Giver of Life"

- The story of the Holy Spirit's work in the world begins not with Pentecost but with the origins of the known universe. It can be seen as a story with four great episodes: the Creator Spirit (1) breathes life into all aspects of the emergence of a life-bearing universe, (2) enfolds human beings in grace, (3) brings about the Christ-event, and (4) is poured out upon the community of disciples, constituting them as church.
- The Creator Spirit is the immanent presence of God to all creatures, breathing life into the whole evolving process of ongoing creation. This Spirit is the power of God at work in the self-transcendence of creation and the emergence of the new.
- The Spirit is the loving companion to every creature and the midwife to the birth of the new. The Spirit is with all creatures in their finitude, death, and incompletion, holding each suffering creature in redemptive love and drawing each into an unforeseeable eschatological future in the divine life.

Ecological Commitment and the Following of Jesus

- In the living memory of the Christian community, Jesus is a Wisdom teacher whose parables are taken from nature, who finds God in the wilderness, and who teaches that God clothes every wildflower and cares for every sparrow that falls to the ground.
- In the light of his resurrection, Jesus is celebrated by the first Christian as the Wisdom/Word of God, the one in whom all things are created and all things are reconciled.

- The contemporary concept of deep incarnation suggests that in the Word made flesh, God has embraced the interconnected world of fleshly creatures, the whole web of life on Earth. The incarnation is God-with-us in the "very tissue" of biological life.
- From the perspective of evolutionary history, Jesus can be seen as the self-transcendence of the evolving universe into God. From the side of God, Jesus can be seen as God's self-communication to creation. Jesus is the event of salvation, because he is both God's self-bestowal to creation and the radical yes of creation to God.

The Diversity of Life and the Trinity

- In a trinitarian theology of creation, everything that exists springs from the divine communion and will find its fulfillment in this communion.
- The word "perichoresis" describes the mutual presence of divine persons, their ecstatic being-with-the-other in diversity and freedom. In this kind of communion, diversity and unity are not opposed but flourish in relation to each other.
- Only the diversity of life—huge soaring trunks of trees, the community of ants, the flashing colors of parrots, the beauty of wildflowers, along with the mind and heart of the human—can give expression to the radical diversity and otherness of the trinitarian God. The diversity of creation, and the diversity of life on Earth, can be seen as sacramental, as expressing and representing the abundance and dynamism of the divine communion.
- The trinitarian insight that God's very being is relational provides a basis for a vision of the fundamental reality of the universe as relational. The interrelatedness that ecologists find in the biosphere on Earth, and the interrelatedness that science discovers at all levels from quantum physics to cosmology, springs from a God whose being is to be in relationship.

The Transformation of All Things in Christ

- The resurrection changes created reality forever. In Jesus' death, he freely hands his bodily existence into the mystery of a loving God. In the resurrection, God adopts Jesus' creaturely reality as God's own reality. The resurrection constitutes an objective change in the world of creatures. It is the promise, and the beginning, of the transformation of all things in Christ.
- We do not have a mental picture of this transformation. The God of the future is a God of radical, incomprehensible mystery. Our future and that of the rest of creation are hidden in God. What we know is the promise of God given in the resurrection of Jesus, a promise that involves the embodied human person and the created universe.
- Based on the God revealed in Christ, individual creatures can be thought of as participating in redemption in Christ by being taken up into the eternal divine life in a way that is appropriate to their nature. This may occur in their being taken up, loved, and celebrated eternally in the living memory of the Trinity and the communion of saints. It may occur in other ways that we cannot yet imagine or envisage.

Worship and Practice

- When Christians gather for Eucharist they bring creation with them. Every Eucharist can be understood as the lifting up of creation to God, the living memory of both creation and redemption, the sacrament of the cosmic Christ, participation with all God's creatures in the communion of the Trinity, and solidarity with victims.
- Following Jesus means following the way of wisdom. It involves seeing all things as loved by God and destined to be taken up and transformed in Christ. It is a call to ecological conversion that

involves a new way of seeing, thinking, and acting. It is a way of loving knowledge, of the "loving eye." It is to be led by the Spirit into ecological praxis, which is a way of seeing that leads to action that leads back to further reflection.

- What is needed is a mysticism of ecological praxis. Politics and mysticism go together. Christians committed to ecological praxis need to be mystics, finding God not only in the experience of the boundless beauty of the natural world but also in the painful dark night of loss, failure, and defeat and in the enduring, life-long commitment to the Earth and its creatures.

Notes

Chapter 1: Introduction

1. This is a theme developed in the pioneering work of Thomas Berry; see his *The Dream of the Earth* (San Francisco: Sierra Club Books, 1988), 11.

2. Pope John Paul II, General Audience Address, January 17, 2001. This idea was taken up in the statement of the Australian Catholic Bishops' Conference *A New Earth: The Environmental Challenge* (Sydney: Australian Catholic Social Justice Council, 2002). On commitment to the integrity of creation as a moral responsibility, see John Paul II, *Sollicitudo Rei Socialis: On Social Concerns* (Homebush, NSW: St Paul Publications, 1988), 74, par. 34; *Message for the Celebration of the World Day of Prayer for Peace* (January 1, 1990), entitled *Peace with God the Creator: Peace with All of Creation* (Homebush, NSW: St Paul Publications, 1990), 5; *The Gospel of Life: Evangelium Vitae* (Homebush, NSW: St Paul's, 1995), 80 par. 42. See also *Centesimus Annus: On the Hundredth Anniversary of Rerum Novarum* (Homebush, NSW: St. Paul Publications, 1991), 70-72, par. 37-38.

3. See Thomas Berry, *Dream of the Earth*, 87, 126; see also Brian Swimme and Thomas Berry, *The Universe Story: From the Primordial Flaring Forth to the Ecozoic Era—A Celebration of the Unfolding of the Cosmos* (San Francisco: HarperSanFrancisco, 1992).

4. See Matthew Fox, *Original Blessing: A Primer in Creation Spirituality* (Santa Fe, N.M.: Bear, 1983), 316-19; see also *The Coming of the Cosmic Christ: The Healing of Mother Earth and the Birth of a Global Renaissance* (New York: Harper and Row, 1988).

5. H. Paul Santmire, *Nature Reborn: The Ecological and Cosmic Promise of Christian Theology* (Minneapolis: Fortress Press, 2000). See also his *The Travail of Nature: The Ambiguous Ecological Promise of Christian Theology* (Philadelphia: Fortress, 1985).

6. My own focus has been on areas of systematic theology with which I am most familiar. For broader approaches to an ecological theology, see Brennan R. Hill, *Christian Faith and the Environment: Making Vital Connections* (Maryknoll, N.Y.: Orbis Books, 1988); John Carmody, *Ecology and Religion: Towards a New Christian Theology of Nature* (New York: Paulist, 1983); John Haught, *The Promise of Nature: Ecology and Cosmic Purpose*

(New York: Paulist, 1993); Celia E. Deane-Drummond, *A Handbook in Theology and Ecology* (London: SCM, 1996); *Creation through Wisdom: Theology and the New Biology* (Edinburgh: T&T Clark, 2000). See also the important attempts at an unambiguously Christian ecological theology in the works of H. Paul Santmire mentioned in the previous note; David Toolan, *At Home in the Cosmos* (Maryknoll, N.Y.: Orbis Books, 2001); Cho Hyun-Chul, S.J., *An Ecological Vision of the World: Towards a Christian Ecological Theology for Our Age* (Rome: Editrice Pontificia Università Gregoriana, 2004); Peter Scott, *A Political Theology of Nature* (Cambridge: Cambridge University Press, 2003). Sean McDonagh has long called the church to ecological conversion. See his *To Care for the Earth: A Call to a New Theology* (Sante Fe, N.M.: Bear, 1986); *The Greening of the Church* (Maryknoll, N.Y.: Orbis Books, 1990); *Passion for the Earth* (Maryknoll, N.Y.: Orbis Books, 1994); *The Death of Life: The Horror of Extinction* (Dublin: Columba Press, 2004). For summaries, see John Hart, *What Are They Saying about Environmental Theology* (New York: Paulist, 2004); and Robert Barry Leal, *The Environment and Christian Faith* (Strathfield, N.S.W.: St Paul's, 2004). See also Dieter T. Hessel and Rosemary Radford Ruether, eds., *Christianity and Ecology: Seeking the Well-Being of Earth and Humans* (Cambridge, Mass.: Harvard University Press, 2000). The task of rethinking Christian theology in terms of ecology is enormous. Ernst Conradie has outlined the scope of this project. See his *Ecological Theology: A Guide for Further Research* (Bellville, South Africa: Publications of the University of the Western Cape, 2001). For a full bibliography, see his *Ecological Theology: An Indexed Bibliography* (Bellville, South Africa: Publications of the University of the Western Cape, 2001).

7. Others have made important contributions to an ecological ethics. Celia Dean-Drummond, for example, argues persuasively for an ethics of nature that builds on a virtue ethic centered on wisdom. See her *The Ethics of Nature* (Oxford: Blackwell, 2004). See also, among many others, Holmes Rolston III, *Environmental Ethics* (Philadelphia: Temple University Press, 1988); James A. Nash, *Loving Nature: Ecological Integrity and Christian Responsibility* (Nashville: Abingdon, 1991); and Larry L. Rasmussen, *Earth Community, Earth Ethics* (Maryknoll, N.Y.: Orbis Books, 1996).

Chapter 2: Human Beings within the Community of Life

1. The observable universe is the universe to which we have empirical access. Some cosmologists work with models that suggest that the

processes that brought our universe into existence from a primordial quantum configuration would also have generated universe regions beyond our observable universe. This would mean that our observable universe would be part of a much larger universe or ensemble of universes.

2. Brian Greene, *The Fabric of the Cosmos* (London: Penguin, 2004), 272.

3. Martin Rees, "Life in Our Universe and Others," in *When Worlds Converge: What Science and Religion Tell Us about the Story of the Universe and Our Place in It,* ed. Clifford N. Matthews, Mary Evelyn Tucker, and Philip Hefner (Chicago/La Salle, Ill.: Open Court, 2002), 30-31. Rees says the story of the early universe is as well founded as what geologists and paleontologists tell us about the early history of the Earth. He points out that it is not size but complexity that makes things hard to understand. The biology of an insect is more complex and difficult to understand than the physics of a star. See his *Before the Beginning: Our Universe and Others* (London: Simon & Schuster, 1997), 62-65.

4. John Barrow, *The Universe That Discovered Itself* (Oxford: Oxford University Press, 2000), 397.

5. George V. Coyne and Alessandro Omizzolo, *Wayfarers in the Cosmos: The Human Quest for Meaning* (New York: Crossroad, 2002), 125.

6. Martin Rees, *Before the Beginning: Our Universe and Others* (London: Touchstone, 1997), 19.

7. John Gribbin, *Stardust: The Cosmic Recycling of Stars, Planets and People* (London: Penguin, 2001), 178.

8. I am reflecting here on the "weak" form of the anthropic principle, which simply brings out the relationship between the fact of the existence of human beings and the constraints that this puts on the nature of the universe. On "anthropic reasoning," see Rees, *Before the Beginning*, 235-69. For a full treatment of the anthropic principle, see J. D. Barrow and F. Tipler, *The Anthropic Cosmological Principle* (Oxford: Oxford University Press, 1986).

9. Ernst Mayr, *What Evolution Is* (London: Weidenfeld and Nicolson, 2001), 47.

10. For the development of this tradition in the patristic writers, see Peter C. Phan, *Grace and the Human Condition* (Wilmington, Del.: Michael Glazier, 1988), 48-54, 125-38.

11. Karl Rahner, *Foundations of Christian Faith* (New York: Seabury, 1978), 189.

12. Claus Westermann, *Creation* (Philadelphia: Fortress, 1974), 58.

13. See Karl Barth, *Church Dogmatics* III, I (Edinburgh: T&T Clark, 1958), 184-85.

14. For the most important texts of the Second Vatican Council on this theme, see the Dogmatic Constitution on the Church (*Lumen Gentium*), par. 16, and the Pastoral Constitution on the Church in the Modern World (*Gaudium et Spes*), par. 22. For Karl Rahner's theology, see his *Foundations of Christian Faith*, 116-33.

15. See, e.g., John Zizioulas, "Preserving God's Creation: Three Lectures on Theology and Ecology," *King's Theological Review* 12 (1989): 1-5, 41-45; 13 (1990): 1-5.

16. This is the translation of *The New American Bible* (Wichita, Kan.: Catholic Bible Publishers, 1970).

17. The complexity of the biblical material has been intensively studied and interpreted from the perspective of the Earth in the Earth Bible project led by my colleague Norman Habel. See, e.g., Norman Habel, "Geophany: The Earth Story in Genesis I," in *The Earth Story in Genesis*, vol. 2 of *The Earth Bible*, ed. Norman C. Habel and Shirley Wurst (Sheffield: Sheffeld Academic Press, 2000), 34-48.

18. Lynn White, "The Historical Roots of Our Ecological Crisis," *Science* 155 (1967): 1203-7.

19. John Paul II, *Sollicitudo Rei Socialis* (encyclical, 1988), 34. See also his *World Day of Prayer for Peace* (January 1, 1990).

20. Arne Naess, "The Shallow and the Deep, Long-Range Ecology Movement: A Summary," *Inquiry* 16 (Spring 1973): 95-100.

21. See Roger Sorrell, *St. Francis of Assisi and Nature: Tradition and Innovation in Western Attitudes towards the Environment* (Oxford: Oxford University Press, 1988), 114, 124.

22. Wali Fejo, "The Voice of the Earth: An Indigenous Reading of Genesis 9," in *Earth Story in Genesis*, ed. Habel and Wurst, 140.

23. Ian G. Barbour, "Scientific and Religious Perspectives on Sustainability," in *Christianity and Ecology: Seeking the Well-Being of Earth and Humans*, ed. Dieter T. Hessel and Rosemary Radford Ruether (Cambridge, Mass.: Harvard University Press, 2000), 388.

24. This is what Santmire calls the "I–Ens relationship." See H. Paul Santmire, *Nature Reborn: The Ecological and Cosmic Promise of Christian Theology* (Minneapolis: Fortress, 2000), 61-73.

25. Rosemary Radford Ruether, "Ecofeminism: The Challenge to Theology," in *Christianity and Ecology*, 104.

26. Elizabeth A. Johnson, *Women, Earth, and Creator Spirit* (New York/Mahwah, N.J.: Paulist, 1993), 39.

27. Dawn M. Nothwehr, *Mutuality: A Formal Norm for Christian Social Ethics* (San Francisco: Catholic Scholars Press, 1998).

28. Rosemary Radford Ruether argues that when human beings make use of other creatures and exercise their covenantal role as caretakers, they should do this only within a larger sensibility of kinship, "rooted in the encounter with nature as 'thou,' as fellow beings each with its own integrity" (*Gaia and God: An Ecofeminist Theology of Earth Healing* [San Francisco: HarperSanFrancisco, 1992], 227-28).

Chapter 3: The Creator Spirit

1. Judith and the Wisdom of Solomon are recognized as part of the canon of scripture as "deuterocanonical" by Roman Catholic and Orthodox churches and as apocryphal by Protestant churches.

2. Paul contrasts the letter of the law with "*the Spirit that gives life*" (2 Cor 3:6). He tells his readers: "The law of *the Spirit of life* in Christ Jesus has set you free from the law of sin and death" (Rom 8:2). He sees the Spirit we have received as a spirit of adoption (Rom 8:15, 23) into the life of God.

3. Irenaeus, *Against Heresies* 5.28.4 (*Ante-Nicene Fathers* [repr., Grand Rapids: Eerdmans, 2001], 1:557—hereafter *ANF*). For some other examples, see *Against Heresies* 4, Pref. 4 (*ANF* 1:463); 4.20.1 (*ANF* 1:487); 5.6.1 (*ANF* 1:531).

4. Ambrose, *Holy Spirit* 2.5.41 (*The Fathers of the Church* [Washington, D.C.: Catholic University of America Press, 1963], 44:110—hereafter *FC*).

5. Stephen Hawking, *A Brief History of Time: From the Big Bang to Black Holes* (New York: Bantam, 1988), 174.

6. Pope John Paul II, *Dominum et Vivificantem* (encyclical), 53. Translated as *The Holy Spirit in the Life of the Church* (Boston: St. Paul, 1986), 91. See also his *Redemptoris Missio,* 28-29.

7. Walter Kasper, *Jesus the Christ* (New York: Paulist, 1976), 251.

8. Ambrose, *The Holy Spirit* 2.5.41 (*FC* 44:110).

9. Yves Congar, *The Word and the Spirit* (London: Geoffrey Chapman, 1986), 87.

10. Yves Congar, *I Believe in the Holy Spirit,* 3 vols. (New York: Seabury, 1983), 2:7.

11. Ibid., 1:156; idem, *Word and the Spirit,* 66-67.

12. Yves Congar, "Pneumatology Today," *American Ecclesiastical Review* 167 (1973): 443.

13. Jürgen Moltmann, *The Spirit of Life: A Universal Affirmation* (Minneapolis: Fortress, 1992), 10.

14. Karl Rahner, *Foundations of Christian Faith* (New York: Seabury, 1978), 178-203.

15. Walter Kasper, *The God of Jesus Christ* (London: SCM, 1983), 227.

16. Wolfhart Pannenberg, *Systematic Theology*, vol. 2 (Grand Rapids: Eerdmans, 1994), 32.

17. Kasper, *God of Jesus Christ*, 195.

18. Ruth Page, *God and the Web of Creation* (London: SCM, 1996), 71.

19. Rosemary Radford Ruether, *Gaia and God: An Ecofeminist Theology of Earth Healing* (San Francisco: HarperSanFrancisco, 1992), 227-28.

20. Moltmann, *Spirit of Life*, 12.

Chapter 4: Ecological Commitment and the Following of Jesus

1. C. H. Dodd, *The Parables of the Kingdom* (Glasgow: Collins, 1961), 20-21.

2. This is a theme of Edward Schillebeeckx in *Jesus: An Experiment in Christology* (New York: Seabury, 1979).

3. See Larry W. Hurtado, *Lord Jesus Christ: Devotion to Jesus in Earliest Christianity* (Grand Rapids: Eerdmans, 2003).

4. For a good summary of the evidence, see Raymond E. Brown, *The Gospel According to John, I-XII* (Garden City, N.Y.: Doubleday, 1966), cxxii-cxxiii, 519-24.

5. See, e.g., Elisabeth Schüssler Fiorenza, *Jesus: Miriam's Child, Sophia's Prophet* (New York: Continuum, 1994).

6. See Elizabeth Johnson, "Jesus the Wisdom of God: A Biblical Basis for a Non-androcentric Christology," in *Ephemerides Theologicae Lovanienses* 41 (1985): 261-94; *She Who Is: The Mystery of God in Feminist Theological Discourse* (New York: Crossroad, 1992); "Wisdom Was Made Flesh and Pitched Her Tent among Us," in *Reconstructing the Christ Symbol: Essays in Feminist Christology*, ed. Maryanne Stevens (New York: Paulist, 1993), 95-117; "Redeeming the Name of Christ," in *Freeing Theology: The Essentials of Theology in Feminist Perspective*, ed. Catherine LaCugna (San Francisco: HarperSanFrancisco, 1993), 115-37.

7. I have developed the idea of wisdom Christology as an ecological theology in *Jesus the Wisdom of God: An Ecological Theology* (Maryknoll, N.Y.: Orbis Books, 1995).

8. Duncan Reid, "Enfleshing the Human," in *Earth Revealing—Earth Healing: Ecology and Christian Theology*, ed. Denis Edwards (Collegeville, Minn.: Liturgical Press, 2001), 69-83.

9. Neil Darragh, *At Home in the Earth* (Auckland: Accent Publications, 2000), 124.

10. Niels Henrik Gregersen, "The Cross of Christ in an Evolutionary World," *Dialog: A Journal of Theology* 40 (2001): 205.

11. See Karl Rahner, "Christology within an Evolutionary View of the World," in *Theological Investigations*, vol. 5 (London: Darton, Longman & Todd, 1966), 157-92. See also his *Foundations of Christian Faith* (New York: Seabury, 1978), 178-223.

12. For this early Franciscan theology, see Ilia Delio, "Revisiting the Franciscan Doctrine of Christ," *Theological Studies* 64 (2003): 3-23.

13. Rahner, *Foundations of Christian Faith*, 197.

14. Ibid., 178-203.

Chapter 5: The Diversity of Life and the Trinity

1. Thomas Aquinas, *Summa Theologiae*, 1.28.2,4.

2. Vladimir Lossky, *Orthodox Theology: An Introduction* (Crestwood, N.Y.: St. Vladimir's Seminary Press, 1978), 43.

3. Bonaventure uses the Latin *circumincessio*, literally to move to and around another. See, e.g., Bonaventure's *Itinerarium Mentis in Deum* 6.2. *Circumincessio* is a dynamic word, suggesting movement and bringing to mind the image of the dance. Other Latin theologians use *circuminsessio*, literally, "to sit or to dwell in and around another."

4. John D. Zizioulas, *Being as Communion: Studies in Personhood and the Church* (Crestwood, N.Y.: St. Vladimir's Seminary Press, 1993), 17.

5. Lossky, *Orthodox Theology*, 43.

6. John Zizioulas, "Human Capacity and Human Incapacity: A Theological Exploration of Personhood," *Scottish Journal of Theology* 28 (1975): 409.

7. Zizioulas, *Being as Communion*, 17; see also idem, "The Doctrine of the Holy Trinity: The Significance of the Cappadocian Contribution," in *Trinitarian Theology Today,* ed. Christoph Schwobel (Edinburgh: T&T Clark, 1995), 44-60.

8. Boris Bobrinskoy, *The Mystery of the Trinity: Trinitarian Experience and Vision in the Biblical and Patristic Tradition* (Crestwood, N.Y.: St. Vladimir's Seminary Press, 1999), 5.

9. Walter Kasper, *The God of Jesus Christ* (New York: Paulist, 1976), 280. This leads him to argue for a view of reality "in which person and relation have priority" (p. 310).

10. Catherine Mowry LaCugna, *God for Us: The Trinity and Christian*

Life (San Francisco: HarperSanFrancisco, 1991), 250. She argues for what she calls an ontology of relation, an understanding that reality is relational to the core. What is needed, she says, is an understanding of being as "being-in-relation not being-in-itself" (p. 246).

11. Elizabeth A. Johnson, *She Who Is: The Mystery of God in Feminist Theological Discourse* (New York: Crossroad, 1992), 22.

12. Jürgen Moltmann, *The Trinity and the Kingdom of God* (London: SCM, 1981), 109.

13. Colin E. Gunton, *The One, the Three and the Many: God, Creation and the Culture of Modernity* (Cambridge: Cambridge University Press, 1993), 230.

14. Colin E. Gunton, *The Promise of Trinitarian Theology* (Edinburgh: T&T Clark, 1991), 164-65.

15. Graham Buxton, *The Trinity, Creation and Pastoral Ministry: Imaging the Perichoretic God* (Milton Keynes, UK: Paternoster, 2005), 195.

16. Bonaventure, *Breviloquium* 2.11-12. He tells us this likeness exists at three levels: "as a trace (*vestigium*), an image, and a likeness. The aspect of trace is found in every creature; the aspect of image, in the intellectual creatures or rational spirits; the aspect of likeness, only in those who are God-conformed."

17. Bonaventure, *Hexaemeron* 13.14.

18. Aquinas, *Summa Theologiae* 1.47.1. See also the *Summa Contra Gentiles* 2.45.2.

19. Belden C. Lane, "Biodiversity and the Holy Trinity," *America* 185, no. 20 (Dec. 17, 2001): 10.

20. Arthur Peacocke, *Theology for a Scientific Age: Being and Becoming—Natural, Divine and Human* (Minneapolis: Fortress, 1993), 38.

21. William R. Stoeger, "The Mind-Brain Problem, the Laws of Nature, and Constitutive Relationships," in *Neuroscience and the Person: Scientific Perspectives on Divine Action,* ed. Robert John Russell, Nancey Murphy, Theo C. Meyering, and Michael Arbib (Vatican City State: Vatican Observatory; Berkeley, Calif.: Center for Theology and the Natural Sciences, 1999), 136-37.

22. Zizioulas, *Being as Communion*, 17.

Chapter 6: The Final Transformation of All Things

1. For an introduction to Teilhard's life, see Ursula King, *Spirit of Fire: The Life and Vision of Teilhard de Chardin* (Maryknoll, N.Y.: Orbis Books,

1996). See also Claude Cuenot, *Teilhard de Chardin: A Biographical Study* (Baltimore: Helicon, 1965); and Robert Speaight, *The Life of Teilhard de Chardin* (New York: Harper and Row, 1967). N. M. Wildiers offers a helpful introduction to Teilhard's thought in his *An Introduction to Teilhard de Chardin* (London: Fontana, 1969).

2. Pierre Teilhard de Chardin, *The Human Phenomenon* (Brighton: Sussex Academic, 1999, 2003), 209-15.

3. Pierre Teilhard de Chardin, *Le Milieu Divin: An Essay on the Interior Life* (London: Fontana, 1965), 123.

4. King, *Spirit of Fire*, 110.

5. Teilhard, *Human Phenomenon*, 216-18.

6. Ibid., 202.

7. Christopher Mooney, *Teilhard de Chardin and the Mystery of Christ* (London: Collins, 1966).

8. See, e.g., the articles by James W. Skeehan, André Daleux, Siôn Cowell, Ursula King, Thomas M. King, Diarmuid O'Murchù, John A. Grim and Mary Evelyn Tucker, Mary Grey, Robert Faricy, Ludovico Galleni and Francesco Scalfari, Celia Deane-Drummond and Richard W. Kropf in *Ecotheology* 10, no. 1 (April 2005) and *Ecotheology* 10, no. 2 (August 2005).

9. At the end of his life, in an article outlining an agenda for Christology, Rahner continued to identify the need to develop the thought of Teilhard de Chardin with more precision and clarity, in order to show the intelligible and orthodox connection between Jesus of Nazareth and Christ as the Omega Point of world evolution. See his "Christology Today," *Theological Investigations,* vol. 21 (New York: Crossroad, 1988), 227. In another article entitled "The Christian Understanding of Redemption" in the same volume, he points to the need for a soteriology that is worked out in relation to contemporary cosmology (p. 252).

10. See Michael W. Petty, *A Faith That Loves the Earth: The Ecological Theology of Karl Rahner* (Lanham, Md.: University Press of America, 1996).

11. Karl Rahner, "Dogmatic Questions on Easter," in *Theological Investigations,* vol. 4 (New York: Seabury, 1966, 1974), 126; see also idem, "Resurrection," in *Encyclopedia of Theology: A Concise Sacramentum Mundi,* ed. Karl Rahner (London: Burns and Oats, 1975), 1438-42.

12. Rahner, "Dogmatic Questions on Easter," 128.

13. Ibid., 129.

14. Karl Rahner, "Natural Science and Reasonable Faith," in *Theological Investigations,* vol. 21, 51; and *Foundations of Christian Faith* (New York: Seabury, 1978), 445-46.

15. Rahner, "Resurrection," 1142.

16. Ibid.

17. Karl Rahner, "The Eternal Significance of the Humanity of Jesus for our Salvation," in *Theological Investigations,* vol. 3 (New York: Seabury, 1974), 43.

18. Karl Rahner, "Hidden Victory," in *Theological Investigations,* vol. 7 (New York: Herder & Herder, 1971), 156.

19. See Karl Rahner, "The Question of the Future," in *Theological Investigations,* vol. 12 (London: Darton, Longmann and Todd, 1974), 181-201.

20. See Karl Rahner, "The Hermeneutics of Eschatological Assertions," *Theological Investigations,* vol. 4, 323-46.

21. Karl Rahner, "The Resurrection of the Body," in *Theological Investigations,* vol. 2 (Baltimore: Helicon, 1963), 213.

22. Karl Rahner, "The Theological Problems Entailed in the Idea of 'The New Earth,'" in *Theological Investigations,* vol. 10 (London: Darton, Longman & Todd, 1973), 260-72.

23. Ibid., 270.

24. Karl Rahner, "Immanent and Transcendent Consummation of the World," in *Theological Investigations,* vol. 10, 289.

25. Karl Rahner, "The Festival of the Future of the World," in *Theological Investigations,* vol. 7, 184.

26. Ibid., 183.

27. See, e.g., the articles in three recent volumes: John Polkinghorne and Michael Welker, eds., *The End of the World and the Ends of God: Science and Theology on Eschatology* (Harrisburg, Pa.: Trinity Press International, 2000); Ted Peters, Robert John Russell, and Michael Welker, eds., *Resurrection: Theological and Scientific Assessments* (Grand Rapids: Eerdmans, 2002); George F. R. Ellis, ed., *Eschatology from a Cosmic Perspective* (Philadelphia: Templeton Foundation, 2002). Robert John Russell has been pursuing this topic; see, e.g., his "Bodily Resurrection, Eschatology, and Scientific Cosmology: The Mutual Interaction of Christian Theology and Science," in *Resurrection: Theological and Scientific Assessments,* 3-30, and his "Eschatology and Physical Cosmology: A Preliminary Reflection," in *Far Future Universe,* 266-315.

28. Jay McDaniel, *Of God and Pelicans: A Theology of Reverence for Life* (Louisville: Westminster John Knox, 1989), 41-47. McDaniel insists that any fulfillment of a pelican can only be one that is appropriate to the nature of a pelican.

29. Ernst Conradie proposes a metaphor of "material inscription,"

where the whole history of the cosmos is not only held in the mind of God, but is also inscribed or fixated in the dimensions of space and time so that the goodness of the material creation is affirmed forever. See E. M. Conradie, "Resurrection, Finitude and Ecology," in *Resurrection: Theological and Scientific Assessments*, 277-96.

30. See Dirk Evers, "Memory in the Flow of Time and the Concept of Resurrection," in *Resurrection: Theological and Scientific Assessments*, 239-54.

31. John F. Haught, *God after Darwin: A Theology of Evolution* (Boulder, Colo.: Westview, 2000), 43. Process philosopher Alfred North Whitehead proposed what he called "objective immortality," the idea that creatures make an impression on God and that this impact remains in God beyond death. See his *Process and Reality: An Essay in Cosmology* (New York: Harper & Row, 1929, 1957), 526-33.

32. Jürgen Moltmann, *The Way of Jesus Christ: Christology in Messianic Dimensions* (London: SCM, 1990), 303.

33. Elizabeth A. Johnson, *Friends of God and Prophets: A Feminist Theological Reading of the Communion of Saints* (London: SCM, 1998), 201.

Chapter 7: Worship and Practice

1. John Zizioulas, "Preserving God's Creation: Three Lectures on Ecology and Theology," *King's Theological Review* 12 (1989): 1-5, 41-45; 13 (1990): 1-5.

2. On this see Patricia A. Fox, *God as Communion: John Zizioulas, Elizabeth Johnson, and the Retrieval of the Symbol of God* (Collegeville, Minn.: Liturgical Press, 2001), 70.

3. Zizioulas says: "All this involves an *ethos* that the world needs badly in our time. Not an ethic, but an *ethos*. Not a program, but an attitude and a mentality. Not legislation, but a culture" ("Preserving God's Creation," *King's Theological Review* 13 [1990]: 5).

4. Louis Bouyer, *Life and Liturgy* (London: Sheed and Ward, 1956), 15-28.

5. Ibid., 132.

6. Zizioulas, "Preserving God's Creation," 4.

7. For the sake of brevity, I will restrict my examples to current Roman Catholic liturgical texts. Further examples can be found in the liturgical texts and hymns of other Christian communities.

8. See Yves Congar's remarks on the doxology in his *I Believe in the Holy Spirit* (New York: Seabury, 1983), 2:224.

9. Karl Rahner, "Dogmatic Questions on Easter," in *Theological Investigations*, vol. 4 (New York: Seabury, 1974), 129.

10. Pierre Teilhard de Chardin, "The Mass on the World," in *Hymn of the Universe* (London: Collins, 1965), 20, 23. On this see Thomas M. King, *Teilhard's Mass: Approaches to "The Mass on the World"* (New York: Paulist, 2005); see also Mary Grey, "Cosmic Communion: A Contemporary Reflection on the Eucharistic Vision of Teilhard de Chardin," *Ecotheology* 10 (2005): 165-80.

11. Teilhard, "Mass on the World," 24.

12. Tony Kelly, *The Bread of God: Nurturing a Eucharistic Imagination* (Melbourne: HarperCollins, 2001), 92.

13. Ibid., 100-101.

14. Johann Baptist Metz, *Faith in History and Society: Towards a Practical Fundamental Theology* (London: Burns and Oates, 1980), 109.

15. *Solidarity with Victims of Climate Change: Reflections on the World Council of Churches' Response to Climate Change* (Geneva: World Council of Churches, 2002), 10.

16. Ibid., 10.

17. Peter Scott, *A Political Theology of Nature* (Cambridge: Cambridge University Press, 2003), 246.

18. Brennan R. Hill, *Christian Faith and the Environment: Making Vital Connections* (Maryknoll, N.Y.: Orbis Books, 1998), 267.

19. Sean McDonagh, *The Death of Life: The Horror of Extinction* (Dublin: Columba Press, 2004), 151.

20. Celia E. Deane-Drummond, *Creation through Wisdom: Theology and the New Biology* (Edinburgh: T&T Clark, 2000); idem, *The Ethics of Nature* (Oxford: Blackwell, 2004). While I recognize that Wisdom can refer to a divine attribute possessed by all three trinitarian persons, my approach is focused on Wisdom as a way of speaking of the eternal hypostasis that is made flesh in Jesus of Nazareth. See Denis Edwards, *Jesus the Wisdom of God: An Ecological Theology* (Maryknoll, N.Y.: Orbis Books, 1995).

21. In Colossians we are told that all the treasures of the wisdom of God are found in Christ (Col 2:3). True wisdom is to be filled with the knowledge of God's promise so as to lead lives worthy of the risen Christ and to bear fruit in good work (Col 1:9-10).

22. Bonaventure, *Hexaemeron* 12; *Itinerarium* 2.12.

23. See Thomas Aquinas, *Summa Theologiae* 1.43.5 ad 2.

24. Sallie McFague, *Super, Natural Christians: How We Should Love Nature* (Minneapolis: Fortress, 1997), 116.

25. Thomas Berry, *The Great Work: Our Way into the Future* (New York: Bell Tower, 1999), 2.

26. David Toolan, *At Home in the Cosmos* (Maryknoll, N.Y.: Orbis Books, 2001), 236.

27. Ibid., 215.

28. Ibid.

29. McDonagh, *Death of Life*, 150.

30. H. Paul Santmire, *Nature Reborn: The Ecological and Cosmic Promise of Christian Theology* (Minneapolis: Fortress, 2000), 119-20.

31. *Let the Many Coastlands Be Glad: A Pastoral Letter on the Great Barrier Reef by the Catholic Bishops of Queensland* (Sydney: Catholic Earthcare Australia, 2004).

32. *The Gift of Water: A Statement from Catholic Earthcare Australia Endorsed by Bishops of the Murray-Darling Basin* (Sydney: Catholic Earthcare Australia, 2004).

33. See, e.g., Karl Rahner, "Christian Living Formerly and Today," in *Theological Investigations,* vol. 7 (New York: Herder & Herder, 1971), 15.

34. On all this see Harvey D. Egan, *Karl Rahner: Mystic of Everyday Life* (New York: Crossroad, 1998), esp. 55-79.

35. Edward Schillebeeckx, *Jesus in Our Western Cultures: Mysticism, Ethics and Politics* (London: SCM, 1987), 73.

36. Brennan Hill discusses how ecological commitment involves a return to an ancient Christian tradition of self-denial in a new form of asceticism: "Environmental concerns bring new light to the discussion of authentic self-denial. No doubt we will all have to live more simply if we wish to share our resources, replenish them, and share them with those in need. The new asceticism returns to natural foods that are nourishing and healthy, and it sets aside the processed and 'fast foods' that are harmful to health and wasteful in their excessive packaging. This spirituality returns to making things, and repairing, patching, and refinishing rather than simply discarding. Such self-denial calls for a detachment from gadgets, faddish items, and luxuries. It is conscientious about adequate exercise and proper health care" (*Christian Faith and the Environment,* 249).

37. Ibid., 75.

38. Sallie McFague, *Life Abundant: Rethinking Theology and Economy for a Planet in Peril* (Minneapolis: Fortress, 2000), 209-10.

Index